The AA 100 Walks in
Southeast England

Produced by AA Publishing
© Automobile Association Developments
Limited 2004

Published by AA Publishing (a trading name
of Automobile Association Developments
Limited, whose registered office is
Millstream, Maidenhead, Windsor,
SL4 5GD; registered number 1878835)

Ordnance Survey® This product includes
mapping data licensed
from Ordnance Survey® with the permission
of the Controller of Her Majesty's Stationery
Office.
© Crown copyright 2004. All rights reserved.
Licence number 399221

ISBN 0 7495 4059 1
A01960

A CIP catalogue record for this book is
available from the British Library.

The contents of this book are believed
correct at the time of printing. Nevertheless,
the publishers cannot be held responsible
for any errors or omissions or for changes in
the details given in this book or for the
consequences of any reliance on the
information it provides. We have tried to
ensure accuracy, but things do change and
we would be grateful if readers would advise
us of any inaccuracies they encounter. This
does not affect your statutory rights.

Please write to:
AA Publishing, FH16, Fanum House,
Basing View, Basingstoke RG21 4EA

We have taken all reasonable steps to
ensure that these walks are safe and
achievable by walkers with a realistic level
of fitness. However, all outdoor activities
involve a degree of risk and the publishers
accept no responsibility for any injuries
caused to readers whilst following these
walks. For more advice on using this book
see page 10 and walking safely see page
112. The mileage range shown on the front
cover is for guidance only – some walks may
exceed or be less than these distances.

These routes appear in the *AA Local Walks*
series and *1001 Walks in Britain*.

Visit AA Publishing at ***www.theAA.com***

Colour reproduction by:
Keene Group, Andover
Printed and bound by:
Leo Paper, China

Acknowledgements

Researched and written by David Hancock,
Nick Channer, David Foster, Deborah King
and Rebecca Ford

Picture credits

All images are held in the Automobile
Association's own photo library (AA World
Travel Library) and were taken by the
following photographers:
Front cover D Croucher; 3 D Forss;
5 S&O Matthews; 6/7 J Miller; 8 D Forss;
9tl W Voysey; 9tr T Souter; 9br J Miller;
10tc W Voysey; 10bl R Strange.

*Opposite: Small craft moored on the
River Arun in Sussex are overlooked
by Arundel Castle*

Contents

Above: Pointing the way, Isle of Wight
Page 6: Sweeping views over the magnificent Kent countryside

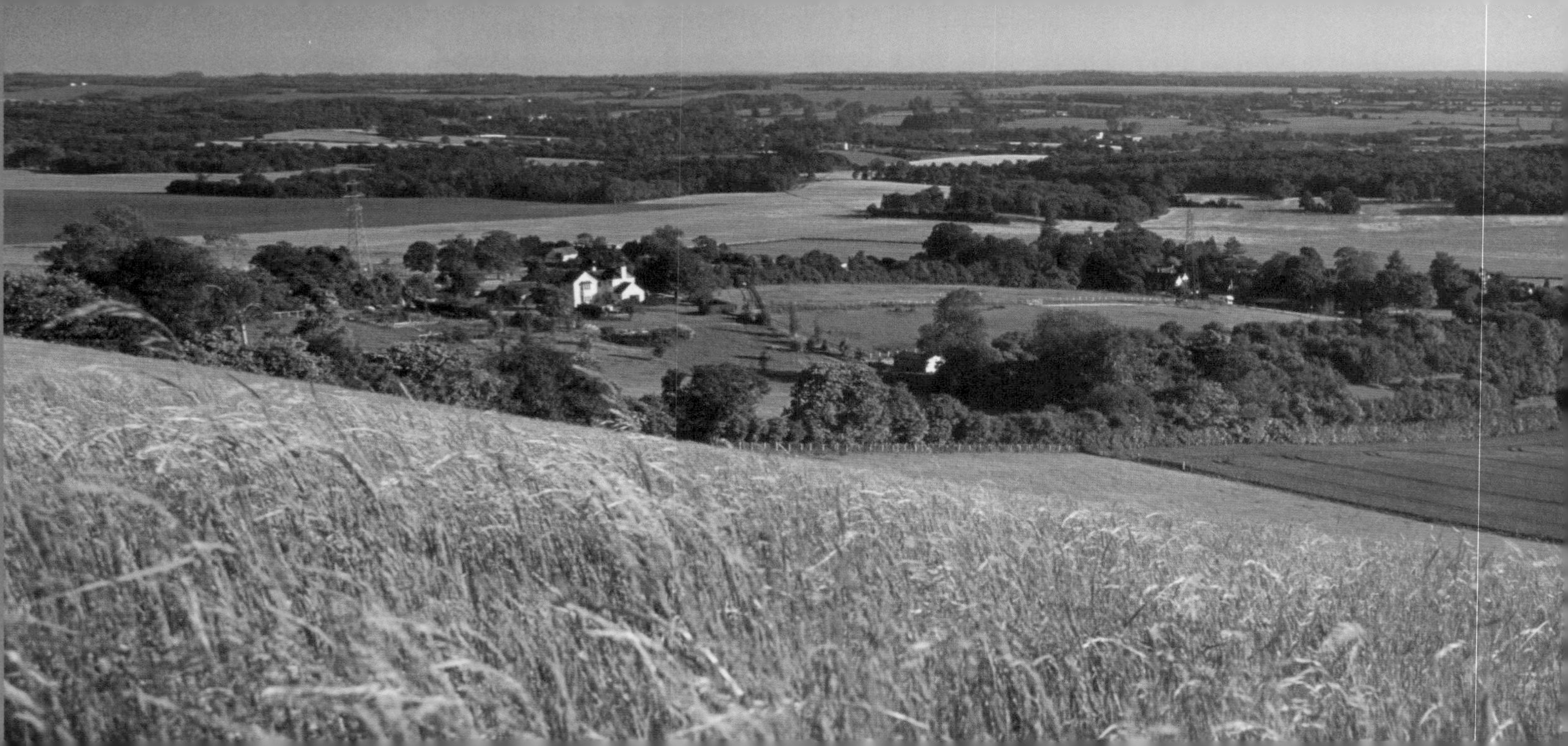

Southeast England

There is an air of industriousness in the southeast. Amid the hustle and bustle there are green oases of peace to discover, a long and complex history to unravel, ancient ways to travel and mysteries to ponder.

7

Southeast England

Chalk downland ridges stretch away to the west; deep beech woods shelter roe deer and muntjac; towering white cliffs form a stunning backdrop along the coast, and lovely thatched villages huddle around a green. And in this region is London – one of the most famous cityscapes in the world. These are a few of the draws of walking in the southeast of England. It's a gentle landscape, essentially agricultural but well wooded in places. Rolling downs and coast have been designated Areas of Outstanding Natural Beauty and there is a network of long distance paths. At its centre are the great parks of London with the Chilterns to the north and west and the downs and estuaries to the south and east. A few hours' travel will take you to the coast – to Hampshire and the Isle of Wight, Sussex and the white cliffs in Kent.

The South Downs and the Isle of Wight

The walks begin on the South Downs, flat-topped chalk hills running from the Sussex coast to Winchester, Alfred's Wessex capital. Leaving this historic townscape by a chalk stream, you climb steeply to a grassy hill, to find the M3 cutting through its heart. Many walks seek out the quiet dells, the ancient woodland and rare heathland tracts. In a corner of Hampshire lies the New Forest, tucked in between bustling seaside Bournemouth and the increasingly industrialised Solent.

The secluded backwater of the Isle

Freshwater Bay, the Isle of Wight

New Forest ponies at Beaulieu

of Wight looks like southern England used to look, without the road schemes and the sprawling suburbs. You can walk its breezy downs in the footsteps of Tennyson or Queen Victoria, or imagine you are a royal prisoner, held in the stronghold of Carisbrooke Castle. Its coastline has cliffs and landslips as dramatic as any in neighbouring Dorset.

A Rich Landscape

Back across the water there are other hills and horizons – Portsdown, one of the great views in Britain; chalk streams and watercress beds; the bizarre line of 'Palmerston's Follies' standing guard to protect the Royal Navy from a landward French assault.

North Hampshire's downs merge into Wiltshire and Berkshire, as you'll find at Ashmansworth and Highclere, but the offshoots of the South Downs, which pile inland towards Alton and Alresford, attain a distinguishing characteristic. This is best discovered with the natural historian Gilbert White, who documented the beech 'hangers' of Selborne in the 18th century. Here you'll also find yourself in the company of Jane Austen (at Chawton) and Alfred, Lord Tennyson and Flora Thompson (at Bramshott).

The wooded South Downs continue east into Sussex, to Black Down, a favourite courting ground for young Victorians, and Goodwood, dominated by the racecourse.

The South Downs Way National Trail traverses the ridge from Winchester to Eastbourne. It's 100 miles (161km) long, but walks here take bite size chunks of it. Climping holds out against the sea and the development that has blighted the rest of the coastline, while Arundel boasts a skyline reminiscent of a French town. Around the back of Brighton, the South Downs continue eastwards, giving breathtaking upland qualities in the deep cutting of the Devil's Dyke. Firle and Arlington are the next stopping off points before you finally make it to the sea.

Now you've made it to real White Cliffs country, though you aren't yet at Dover. In the remote flatlands of Romney Marsh, Rye built fortifications to keep out the raiding French, and at Pevensey the French landed unopposed and won a famous victory at Battle. Dover's famous cliffs served as a wartime bastion against Nazi

Above: The South Downs footpath
Below: Mermaid Street in Rye

Europe, and Julius Caesar was one of many great leaders to camp his army at Barham.

Old Routes

As you begin to explore the northern half of Kent, you will encounter the Pilgrims Way, a medieval route to Canterbury and the shrine of Thomas Becket. For much of the way it follows the line of the North Downs, which are traversed by the North Downs Way.

Kent has always attracted writers, and you will discover connections with Dickens at Rochester and Jane

Austen, who wrote *Pride and Prejudice* at Chilham. H E Bates even gave us a 'perfick' catchphrase to accompany a walk around Pluckley.

The North Downs take us back to the west, skirting the top of the Weald to pause to take the waters at Tunbridge Wells or trace the work of the early ironmasters at Brenchley. Soon you'll be in Surrey, enjoying the view from Box Hill, or the hideaway known as Friday Street. This intricate landscape of downs, woods and scraps of heath is of immeasurable value. Hydon Ball was bought by the National Trust as a monument to Octavia Hill who was instrumental in establishing the Trust as a preserver of habitats and landscapes. Today they protect much of the downland.

Oast houses in Pluckley, Kent

Escaping the Suburbs

You'll discover the wild heath of Chobham Common and the ancient riverside abbey at Waverley. This greenbelt continues around the capital, with the Chilterns in the north. The golden leaves of Burnham Beeches in autumn are particularly striking. Sunningdale has always been a retreat for the rich and infamous – Edward VIII and General Pinochet, to name but two occasional residents. It's an area of heath and wood and large houses. But nothing compares with Windsor Great Park and its deer.

The Capital

To really enjoy the southeast, you must also appreciate the urban environment, and London is special. There is parkland – Regents Park, Hyde Park, Holland Park, Hampstead Heath, Richmond Park – and also the river, and the best way to see Westminster or Mayfair is on foot.

Using this Book

❶ Information panels

Information panels show the total distance and total amount of ascent (that is how much ascent you will accumulate throughout the walk). An indication of the gradient you will encounter is shown by the rating 0–3. Zero indicates fairly flat ground and 3 indicates undulating terrain with several very steep slopes.

❷ Minimum time

The minimum time suggested is for approximate guidance only. It assumes reasonably fit walkers and doesn't allow for stops.

❸ Start points

The start of each walk is given as a six-figure grid reference prefixed by two letters indicating which 100km square of the National Grid it refers to. You'll find more information about grid references on most Ordnance Survey maps.

00 Location Walk title

Country • Region

① 4½ miles (7.2km) 1hr 45min **Ascent:** 131ft (40m) ⚠️

Paths: Cliff top, shingle beach, farm track and country lanes, 1 stile

Suggested map: OS Explorer 231 Southwold & Bungay

Grid reference: TM 522818

Parking: On street near Covehithe church

See the effects of coastal erosion on a walk along a rapidly disappearing cliff top.

① Take tarmac lane from **St Andrew's Church** down towards sea to barrier ('Danger') and sign warning that there is no public right of way. Although this is strictly true, this is well-established and popular path stretching north towards Kessingland beach and you are likely to meet many other walkers. The warnings are serious but it is quite safe to walk here so long as you keep away from the cliff edge.

② Walk through gap to **R** of road barrier and continue towards cliffs. Turn **L** along wide farm track with pig farm to your **L**. Path follows cliff top then descends towards beach to enter **Benacre nature reserve**. On **L** is **Benacre Broad**, once an estuary, now a marshy lagoon. The shingle beach attracts little terns in spring and summer and you should keep to the path to avoid their nesting sites.

③ Climb back on to cliffs at end of Benacre Broad. The way cuts through pine trees and bracken on

constantly changing path before running alongside field and swinging **R** to descend to beach level, where you take wide grass track on your **L** across dunes.

④ At concrete track, with tower of Kessingland church in distance, turn **L** following waymarks of **Suffolk Coast and Heaths Path.** Cross stile and keep straight ahead, passing **Beach Farm** on R. Stay straight ahead for 1 mile (1.6km) on wide track between fields with views of Benacre church ahead.

⑤ Go through white gates and turn **L** on to quiet country lane. Stay on lane for ¾ mile (1.2km) as it passes between hedges with arable farmland to either side and swings **L** at entrance to **Hall Farm.**

⑥ When road bends **R**, turn **L** past gate with an English Nature 'No Entry' sign for cars. Stay on this permissive path as it swings **R** around meadow and continues into woodland of **Holly Grove.** Pass through another gate and turn **L** along road for ¾ mile (1.2km) back into **Covehithe.** Turn **L** at junction to return to **St Andrew's Church.**

④ Abbreviations

Walk directions use these abbreviations:

L – left
L–H – left-hand
R – right
R–H – right-hand

Names which appear on signposts are given in brackets, for example ('Bantam Beach').

⑤ Suggested maps

Details of appropriate maps are given for each walk, and usually refer to 1:25,000 scale Ordnance Survey Explorer maps. We strongly recommend that you always take the appropriate OS map with you. Our hand-drawn maps are there to give you the route and do not show all the details or relief that you will

need to navigate around the routes provided in this collection. You can purchase OS maps at all good bookshops, or by calling Stanfords on 020 7836 2260.

⑥ Car parking

Many of the car parks suggested are public, but occasionally you may find you have to park

on the roadside or in a lay-by. Please be considerate when you leave your car, ensuring that access roads or gates are not blocked and that other vehicles can pass safely. Remember that pub car parks are private and should not be used unless you are visiting the pub or you have the landlord's permission to park there.

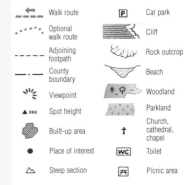

Map legend

←	Walk route	P	Car park
⋯	Optional walk route	〰️	Cliff
– – –	Adjoining footpath		Rock outcrop
	County boundary		Beach
🔆	Viewpoint	🌲	Woodland
▲ 392	Spot height		Parkland
	Built-up area	✝	Church, cathedral, chapel
●	Place of interest	WC	Toilet
△	Steep section	⛱	Picnic area

Bramshott Following Flora's Footsteps

4 miles (6.4km) 2hrs **Ascent:** 295ft (90m)

Paths: Woodland paths and heathland tracks, 3 stiles

Suggested map: OS Explorer 133 Haslemere & Petersfield

Grid reference: SU 855336

Parking: Unsurfaced car park on edge of Bramshott Common

This heath and woodland beauty spot was much loved by writer Flora Thompson.

❶ From car park, take path beyond low wooden barrier. Gradually descend. At bottom, main bridleway (blue arrow) directs you **L** along sunken track. Ignore this if wet and muddy and climb path ahead beneath trees. At fork, keep **L** down to river and footbridge.

❷ Cross bridge. Turn **R** along footpath parallel with river. Pass **wishing well** and house. Proceed through valley bottom to L of 3 **ponds**, to reach lane by ford.

❸ Just before lane, turn **L**, pass memorial stone and steeply ascend through woodland. As it levels out, cross path, then track. Shortly merge with gravel track. Keep **L**, pass bridleway on L, then, where track begins to curve L downhill, keep ahead through trees.

❹ Cross path. In a few paces, at broad sandy track bordering open heathland, turn **R**. On reaching fork, bear **L** over common. Path soon widens and descends to T-junction (fingerpost visible on R at next junction).

❺ Turn **L**. Follow open heathland trail, edged by bracken and gorse, and eventually merge with wider sandy trail. Keep **L** then, on reaching bench and junction of ways on the common fringe, proceed ahead through mixed woodland.

❻ At crossing of paths by line of telegraph poles, turn **L** with bridleway signs. Keep ahead at junction of paths, following bridleway (blue arrow) close to woodland fringe. Stay with telegraph poles, ignoring bridleway R as both merge later. Beyond this point ignore bridleway R; continue to crossing of bridleways.

❼ Turn **R**; keep straight on at next crossing of routes, following footpath marker alongside a garden to stile on woodland edge. Walk along the **L-H** edge of pasture to stile in field corner.

❽ Steeply descend into woodland and cross gravel track to reach stile. At track beyond, turn **R** downhill to river and footbridge encountered on outward route. Retrace your steps back to car park.

The Hangers Looking for Edward Thomas

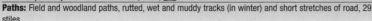

3 miles (4.8km) 2hrs **Ascent:** 682ft (208m) ▲

Paths: Field and woodland paths, rutted, wet and muddy tracks (in winter) and short stretches of road, 29 stiles

Suggested map: OS Explorer 133 Haslemere & Petersfield

Grid reference: SU 746291

Parking: By village green and church in Hawkley

Explore the beech-clad hills and vales that so inspired Hampshire's great poet.

1 With your back to **Hawkley church**, walk **L** beside green to road junction. With **Hawkley Inn** to your **L**, cross straight over down Cheesecombe Farm Lane ('**Hangers Way**'). Shortly, bear off **R** along concrete path. Descend to stile and keep straight on at fork of paths, with **Cheesecombe Farm** to **L**.

2 Cross **Oakshott Stream** and keep **L** along field edge beside woodland. Steeply ascend to stile, keep **R** to further stile, then turn **L** beside fence and drop down to track. Turn **R**, to reach lane, then **R** again for 55yds (50m) to take waymarked right of way beside Wheatham Hill House.

3 Climb long and steep, chalky track up through **Down Hanger** (be warned this gets very wet and muddy), with views unfolding east along the South Downs. At top of **Wheatham Hill**, turn **R** at T-junction

of tracks along **Old Litten Lane**. In 300yds (274m), take **Hangers Way** right over stile. For Edward Thomas memorial stone and South Downs views, continue along track for 200yds (183m) and turn **L** with waymarker. Pass beside wooden barrier and drop down to clearing on **Shoulder of Mutton Hill**.

4 On return route, follow short section of **Hangers Way**, this is a 21-mile (33.6km) long-distance trail that traverses East Hampshire, from Queen Elizabeth Country Park to Alton. Follow trail as it descends through edge of beech woods and steeply down across lush meadowland, eventually joining drive to **Lower Oakshott Farmhouse** and road.

5 Turn **R**, then **L** over stile and follow defined **Hangers Way** path through **Oakshott Valley**, crossing stiles, plank bridges and delightful meadows to reach junction of paths before **Cheesecombe Farm**. Turn **L** to stile and retrace your steps back to **Hawkley**.

13

Chawton Jane Austen's Inspiration

5 miles (8km) 2hrs 30min **Ascent:** 134ft (41m)

Paths: Field paths, old railway track, some road walking, 16 stiles

Suggested map: OS Explorer 133 Haslemere & Petersfield

Grid reference: SU 708375

Parking: Free village car park opposite Jane Austen's House

A gentle ramble around the pastoral countryside that surrounds Chawton.

❶ Turn **L** out of car park, opposite **Jane Austen's House.** Walk along dead-end lane, pass **school,** then **R** into **Ferney Close.** Keeping to **L,** bear **L** along path beside Ferney Bungalow to stile. Continue along **L-H** field edge to stile and cross (with care) **A32.**

❷ Climb steps and stile; walk along **L-H** field edge, leading to stile on **L.** Through copse, following path **R,** then **L** between fields to reach track (**former railway track bed**). Keep ahead at crossing of paths (track now earth and shaded by trees).

❸ On reaching bridge, bear **L** with main path towards silos, path soon passing behind them to reach stile. Cross **A32;** join track leading to **Manor Farm.** At crossing of tracks, by **play area,** turn **R.** Take narrow path **L** at bottom of play area to reach track.

❹ Turn **R** into lane in **Upper Farringdon,** opposite **Massey's Folly.** Turn **L** into churchyard and leave by main gate, turning **L** along lane. Keep ahead along **Gaston Lane** for ½ mile (800m) to track on **L.**

❺ Turn **L** then, shortly, take grassy track **R** to gate; climb stile ahead into open pasture. Keep **R** of brook; cross stile; then bridge over **brook** on **L.** Keep going, with brook to **R,** to stile at end of field.

❻ Turn immediately **L.** Go through gate to join permissive path between fences. Follow it **R,** towards **Whitehouse Farm.** At junction of paths by track, turn **L** through gate and keep to **R-H** field edge to gate.

❼ Bear **R** across field to stiles set in hedge; maintain direction across 3 more fields and stiles towards **Eastfield Farm.** Skirt round farm via yellow-topped squeeze stiles through several fields to reach stile beside woodland, beyond corrugated iron shed.

❽ Go through copse to stile. Bear half-**L** across field to further stile. Continue ahead to stile in wall. Walk along narrow footpath back to main village street. Turn **L** back to car park.

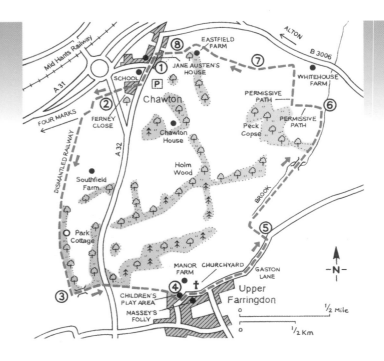

Selborne In the Footsteps of Gilbert White

3½ miles (5.7km) 1hr 30min **Ascent:** 361ft (110m) 🔺

Paths: Woodland, field paths, stretch of metalled road, 7 stiles

Suggested map: OS Explorer 133 Haslemere & Petersfield

Grid reference: SU 741334

Parking: Free National Trust car park behind Selborne Arms

Enjoy the beech hangers that inspired the eminent naturalist.

❶ Take arrowed footpath ('Zig-Zag Path & Hangers') by car park entrance and gently ascend to gate at base of **Selborne Hill** & **Common**. Bear **L** to follow impressive **Zig-Zag** path uphill, pausing at regular intervals to catch your breath and to admire unfolding views across village.

❷ At top, take stepped path **R**. After few paces, keep **R** at fork to follow lower path through beech hangers. Shortly, look out for metal bench, by path ascending from R – savour views. Continue along path, descending to junction of paths, by National Trust sign.

❸ Turn **R** downhill along track then, where this curves L, bear **R** across stile into pasture. Keep to L-H edge, cross 3 more stiles and follow path to lane. Turn **R** and follow it back into village, opposite church. Turn **R** along B3006 road for The Wakes and car park, if you wish to cut walk short.

❹ Cross B road and follow Hangers Way sign through churchyard to gate. Follow defined path to footbridge over **Oakhanger Stream**.

❺ Keep to **Hangers Way** through gate and along edge of meadowland to gate, then pass through stretch of woodland to kissing gate and fork of paths.

❻ Proceed straight ahead (yellow arrow), leaving **Hangers Way**. Eventually pass alongside fence to stile on edge of **Coombe Wood**. Keep close to woodland fringe to stile, then bear **L** along field edge to stile and turn **R** along bridleway towards **Priory Farm**. Keep to track through farmyard to metalled drive.

❼ After few paces, where it curves L, bear **R** along track beside bungalow. Cross stile and follow grassy track uphill along field edge, through gate, eventually reaching gate and woodland. Follow track (can be muddy) through beech woodland. Leave wood, passing house called **Dorton's**, and climb lane steeply back to **Selborne**, turning **L** for car park.

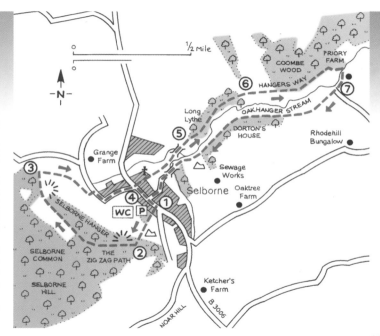

Odiham A Castle and a Canal

4 miles (6.4km) 2hrs **Ascent:** 147ft (45m)
Paths: Canal tow path, field edge and woodland, 20 stiles
Suggested map: OS Explorer 144 Basingstoke, Alton & Whitchurch
Grid reference: SU 740510
Parking: Odiham High Street or signed pay-and-display car parks

A lovely walk combining the elegant country town of Odiham with a castle and the Basingstoke Canal.

❶ Head east along High Street and then take **L** fork, London Road, leading to **Basingstoke Canal**. Pass **Water Witch pub** and cross bridge, then drop down **L** to walk along tow path. Follow waterway parallel with **A287** for just over 1 mile (1.6km) to North Warnborough village.

❷ Pass **Jolly Miller pub** and go under road bridge. Keep to tow path, passing swing bridge, then in 300yds (274m) pass ruins of **Odiham Castle** (or **King John's Castle**) on your R. Pass over **River Whitewater** and continue for ½ mile (800m) to Greywell Tunnel, famous for its roosting bat population and best visited at dusk. Take path **L** over its portal and drop down to road.

❸ Turn **R** into Greywell, then **L** at junction to pass **Fox and Goose pub**. Walk through village and turn **L**

through lychgate to **St Mary's Church**. Walk down path to church and turn **L** through gate opposite. Keep to R-H field edge then, in 200yds (183m), turn **R** to stile and bridge over **River Whitewater** and enter Greywell Moors Nature Reserve.

❹ Walk through wood, passing memorial to the eminent biologist EC Wallace, and keep ahead across 2 stiles in field. Proceed in easterly direction across field to stile and road. Turn **L** for 50yds (46m), then **R** with footpath sign. Walk along **L-H** field edge to stile, then bear diagonally across paddock to stile and maintain direction across next field to further stile.

❺ Cross road to stile opposite and walk across field, heading to **R** of 3 chimneys, to stile. Join path alongside **school** and then turn **R** to **West Street**. Turn **L**, passing **school**, then as road veers L, bear **R** up West Street to roundabout. Go straight over and back along Odiham High Street.

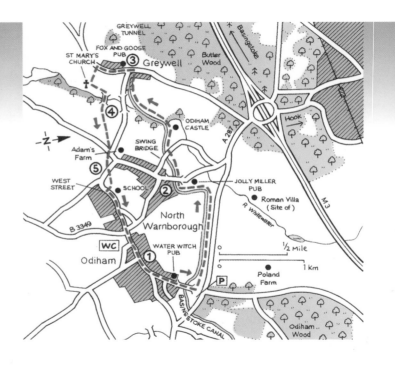

Southwick Ports Down's Fortress Follies

6 miles (9.7km) 3hrs **Ascent:** 390ft (119m)

Paths: Field, woodland paths and stretches of road, 17 stiles
Suggested map: OS Explorer 119 Meon Valley
Grid reference: SU 627085
Parking: Free car park by Southwick Village Hall, close to HMS *Dryad*

A ramble from Southwick to Fort Nelson.

1 From car park, turn **R** to junction and **L** to roundabout. Go straight over, taking narrow lane for **Portchester**. Climb steeply, bearing **R** by quarry then, where road veers sharp L, take lane **R**.

2 Descend for 150yds (137m). Go **L** through gap in hedge. Take footpath diagonally across field, (head just to **R** of Nelson's Monument). Keep ahead across next field to stile and lane. Turn **L**, pass **Nelson's Monument,** then **R** at crossroads ('**Fort Nelson**').

3 Visit fort. Retrace route back to Monument and continue down lane for 50yds (46m). Take footpath **L** over stile. Head towards **R** corner of fort, cross stile and skirt edge of fort to further stile. Bear half-**R** across field, between house and pylon, to road.

4 Turn **R** downhill, then **R** again at next junction. After 200yds (183m) bear **L** through **St Nicholas's churchyard**. Rejoin road; continue past barns and pond. Shortly, beside lay-by, bear **L** over stile. Follow footpath along **L-H** field edge. Continue on between fields, then by **Grub Coppice** to cross bridge.

5 Climb stile, keep to **R-H** field edge to stile on **R**. Cross next stile. Keep to **L-H** field edge to further stile. Turn **L** over stile by stream and bear **R**, around field edge to stile and road. Cross stile opposite. Walk along **R-H** field edge close to stream. Follow field boundary **L**; shortly bear **R** across bridge and stile to join track.

6 Go between farm buildings, through gate and bear **L** to **B2177**. Cross and take footpath **R** on track. It becomes grassy and bears **R** into woodland. Take 2nd footpath **R**, emerge from trees and head across narrow field. Cross bridge, bear **R**, then half-**L** making for large oak. Swing **L** and descend steps to lane.

7 Cross and bear half-**R** across field towards church tower. Cross bridge and continue through plantation. Beyond another bridge, walk up drive to road. Turn **L**, then **R** into Southwick. Keep **L** at junction and **L** again to car park.

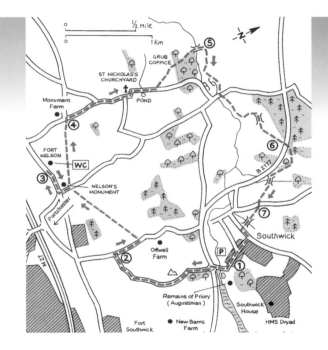

Alresford A Watercress Walk

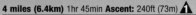

4 miles (6.4km) 1hr 45min **Ascent:** 240ft (73m)	
Paths: Riverside paths, tracks, field, woodland paths and roads	
Suggested map: OS Explorer 132 Winchester	
Grid reference: SU 588325	
Parking: Pay-and-display car park off Station Road, New Alresford	

Exploring New Alresford – the 'new' market town at the heart of Hampshire's watercress industry.

❶ From car park walk down **Station Road** to T-junction with **West Street**. Turn **R** then **L** down **Broad Street**. This is a sumptuous street, which is lined with limes and elegant colour-washed houses. Mary Russell Mitford, authoress of *Our Village*, was born at number 27 in 1787. Keep **L** at bottom of road and proceed along **Mill Lane**. Halfway down follow Wayfarer's Walk marker **L** and soon join river bank and pass **Fulling Mill Cottage** straddling the **River Arle**. It is 300 years old and it was where the homespun wool was scoured and washed, pounded with mallets, stretched, brushed and sheared.

❷ Continue to bottom of Dean Lane and then keep along riverside path. Cross footbridge over **River Arle**, and drop down to pass some cottages. Shortly, cross lane on to wide track and soon follow it as it leads gently downhill to reach junction of tracks. Bear **R** uphill to lane.

❸ Turn **L**, descend to **Fobdown Farm** and take track on **R** beside the farm buildings. On reaching T-junction of tracks, turn **R** and follow established track for just over ½ mile (800m), gently descending into **Old Alresford**.

❹ Pass **watercress beds** on your **R** and follow (now metalled) lane **L**, past houses. Alresford has ideal conditions for growing watercress and is 'Watercress Capital' of England and you'll pass several watercress beds. Turn **R** beside the green to B3046. Cross straight over and follow pavement right to reach lane opposite 18th-century **St Mary's Church**.

❺ After you have visited the church, cross road and turn **L** along pavement to grass triangle by junction. Bear **R** along lane and take footpath ahead over stream and beside watercress beds back to **Mill Lane** and **Broad Street**.

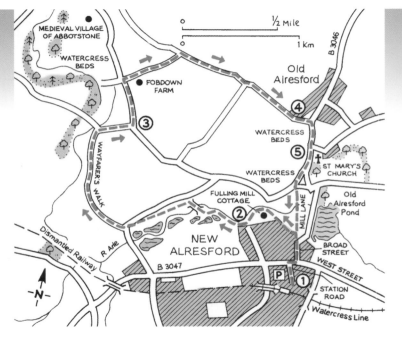

Winchester Alfred's Ancient Capital

3½ miles (5.7km) 1hr 30min **Ascent:** 499ft (152m)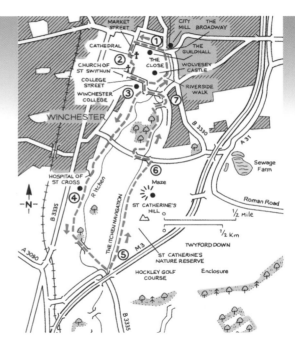

Paths: Established riverside paths through water-meadows, 3 stiles

Suggested map: OS Explorer 132 Winchester

Grid reference: SU 486294

Parking: Pay-and-display car parks in city centre

Winchester's historic streets, Cathedral Close and the beautiful Itchen Valley.

❶ From King Alfred's statue on **Broadway**, walk towards city centre, passing **Guildhall** (tourist information centre) on L. Join High Street, then in 100yds (91m), turn **L** along Market Street. Continue ahead into Cathedral Close to pass cathedral main door.

❷ Turn **L** down cloister, then **R** through Close ('**Wolvesey Castle**'), to Cheyney Court and exit via Prior's Gate. Turn **L** though Kingsgate, with tiny **Church of St Swithun** above, then bear **L** down **College Street** and shortly pass entrance to **Winchester College**. Beyond road barrier, bear **R** along College Walk then turn **R** at end of wall, along track.

❸ Go **L** through gate by private entrance to **College**. Follow path beside **River Itchen** for ½ mile (800m) to gate and road. Cross over and follow gravel path, alongside tributary, to gate and cross open meadow towards **Hospital of St Cross**.

❹ Keep **L** alongside wall and through avenue of trees to stile. Proceed ahead along gravel path to 2 further stiles and join farm track leading to road. Turn **L** and walk length of now gated road (traffic-free), crossing **River Itchen** to reach junction of paths by **M3**.

❺ Turn **L** along path. Pass gate on R (access to **St Catherine's Hill**). Keep **L** at fork and drop down to follow narrow path by **Itchen Navigation**. Go through car park to road.

❻ Turn **L** across bridge and take footpath immediately **R**. Keep to path beside water, disregarding path L (College nature reserve). Soon cross bridge by rowing sheds to join metalled track.

❼ Turn **L**, then **L** again at road. Follow road **L** along College Walk then bear **R** at end ('**Riverside Walk**'). Pass Old Bishops Palace (**Wolvesey Castle**) and follow metalled path beside Itchen and up steps to Bridge Street, opposite **City Mill** (National Trust). Turn **L** back to King Alfred's statue.

Bursledon The Hamble Estuary

6 miles (9.7km) 3hrs **Ascent:** 164ft (50m)

Paths: Riverside, field and woodland paths, some stretches of road

Suggested map: OS Outdoor Leisure 22 New Forest

Grid reference: SU 485067

Parking: Pay-and-display car park by Quay in Hamble

Exploring both sides of the Hamble estuary.

❶ From quayside car park, walk to pontoon and take passenger ferry across estuary to **Warsash** (weather permitting Monday–Friday 7am–5pm; Saturday, Sunday 9am–6pm). Turn **L** along raised gravel path beside estuary and mudflats. Cross footbridge and continue to gravelled parking area. During exceptionally high tides path may flood, so walk through car park and rejoin it by marina.

❷ At **boatyard**, keep **R** of boat shed. Bear **L** beyond, between shed and TS Marina. Bear **R** in front of sales office to rejoin path. Reach lane, turn **L**, pass **Victory Cottages** (R). Continue by **Moody's Boatyard** to A27.

❸ Turn **L** and cross **Bursledon Bridge**. (Turn **R** before bridge to visit **Bursledon Brickworks**.) Pass beneath railway and turn **L** ('the Station'). Turn **L** into Station Road, then **L** again into station car park ('**Jolly Sailor**'). Climb steep path to road. Turn **L** at junction, then **L** again to reach pub.

❹ Return along lane and fork **L** along High Street into Old Bursledon. Pause at excellent **viewpoint** at **Hacketts Marsh**, then bear **L** at **telephone box** along High Street. Pass Vine Inn and **Salters Lane**, then at R bend, bear **L** by Thatched Cottage along footpath.

❺ Join metalled lane by drive to Coach House then, as lane curves L, continue beside house (Woodlands), following path downhill to stream. Proceed uphill through woodland (**Mallards Moor**). At junction of paths on woodland fringe bear **L** with bridleway. At concrete road bear **R**, then **L** to join fenced path.

❻ Cross **railway bridge** and soon pass barrier to road. Keep **L** round sharp L-H bend. Look out for waymarked footpath on **R** and follow path behind houses for ½ mile (800m).

❼ Join metalled path, passing modern housing to road. Follow to Hamble Lane. Turn **L** on to High Street. At roundabout, bear **R** on Lower High Street to Quay and car park.

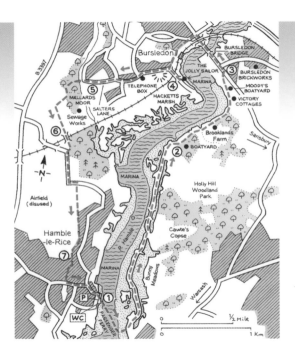

Romsey A Grand Abbey

5½ miles (8.8km) 2hrs 30min **Ascent:** 120ft (40m)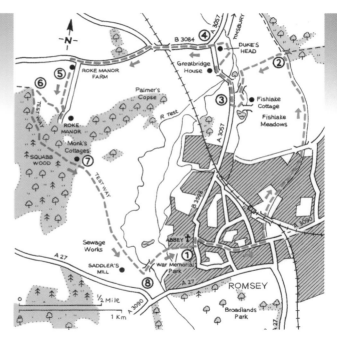

Paths: Tow path, field and woodland paths, some roads, 14 stiles
Suggested map: OS Explorer 131 Romsey, Andover & Test Valley
Grid reference: SU 099666
Parking: Romsey town centre, several pay-and-display car parks

Explore a market town and the Test Valley.

1 From Market Square head east along the Hundred and continue into Winchester Road. At roundabout, turn **L** up steps to join footpath to **Timsbury**. Walk alongside old canal as it passes under railway and then road bridge, and leave town into open meadowland.

2 At crossing of paths (with bridge R), turn **L** and walk along **L-H** field edge. Bear **R** across bridges in corner and follow path beside stream to **River Test**. Turn **L** along river bank, cross wooden bridge and walk alongside opposite bank to stile and track by bridge and house. Turn **R** to **A3057** and turn **R**.

3 Follow pavement and cross **Test**, then take footpath immediately **R** alongside river. Pass bridge, then follow official diversion **L** around house to track. Turn **L** to main road and **Duke's Head** on **L**.

4 Cross road to join **B3084**, ('**Roke Manor**'). Carefully walk along this road, which is often busy (some verges) for ½ mile (800m), then just beyond railway bridge, fork **L** for **Roke Manor**. Pass entrance to **Manor** and take drive on **L**.

5 Pass **Roke Manor Farm**, then on nearing **Manor** bear half-**R** along road for 100yds (91m). Take footpath **R** (can be overgrown) and shortly bear **R** through hedge, then **L** around field. Skirt copse on L to locate **Test Way** sign and turn **L** through gate.

6 Walk into **Squabb Wood** on bracken-lined path, cross 2 plank bridges and reach junction of paths. Keep **L** with **Test Way** and proceed through wood, via plank bridges and stiles, looking out for **Test Way** markers.

7 Leave wood and bear half-**R** across field to stiles and footbridge, then bear slightly **L** to further stiles and footbridge. Keep to **L-H** edge of field, pass through 2 kissing-gates and walk along track to gate. Turn **L** between houses to **River Test** by **Saddler's Mill**.

8 Bear **L** by mill to leave **Test Way**. Cross river; follow tarmac path. Shortly pass **War Memorial Park**. Keep on road close to Abbey back to Market Square.

11 Ashmansworth The Hampshire Highlands

5½ miles (8.8km) 2hrs 30min **Ascent:** 609ft (203m)
Paths: Ridge tracks, field paths and country road
Suggested map: OS Explorers 131 Romsey, Andover & Test Valley; 144 Basingstoke, Alton & Whitchurch
Grid reference: SU 416575
Parking: Along village street by the Plough

Hidden combes and heady heights on the North Hampshire Downs.

❶ Walk north along village street, keeping ahead at fork ('Newbury'). In ¼ mile (400m), just before you reach a house, turn **L** along byway ('**Wayfarer's Walk**'– 'WW'). With superb views unfolding across Berkshire, keep to ancient track along ridge and beside **Bunkhanger Copse** to lane.

❷ Turn **R**. In ¼ mile (400m), bear **L** with **WW** marker, just before lane begins to descend. Follow stony track along ridge, bearing **L** then **R** to cross open downland to crossing of paths.

❸ Cross stile on **L** and head straight across pasture, called **Pilot Hill**, to stile. Bear **L** along field edge, then **R** on to stony track alongside woodland. Steeply descend into combe, keep ahead at crossing of tracks and gradually climb, track eventually merging with metalled lane.

❹ Turn **R** into **Faccombe** and turn **L** along village street. Pass estate office and lane on R ('**Jack Russell Inn**') then turn **L** ('**Ashmansworth**') by the side of **Faccombe Manor**. In 200yds (183m), take arrowed path **L** beside double gates.

❺ Keep to **L-H** field-edge, following track **R**, and steeply descend through woodland. At junction of tracks, bear **R** to pass 2 brick-and-flint farm buildings (**Curzon Street Farm**).

❻ Proceed straight on at crossing of tracks. Keep to main track as it steeply ascends valley side into woodland. Emerge from trees and keep to track beside Privet Copse. Continue ahead at junction of tracks, across field and track to join narrow path (marked by yellow arrow on post) through copse.

❼ Drop down on to track, bear **L**, then immediately **R** and steeply climb to gap beside gate. Turn **L** along lane, following it uphill into **Ashmansworth**.

Highclere Castle Above the Castle

6½ miles (10.4km) 3hrs **Ascent:** 767ft (234m)

Paths: Tracks, field and woodland paths, some roads, 6 stiles
Suggested map: OS Explorers 144 Basingstoke, Alton & Whitchurch; 158 Newbury & Hungerford
Grid reference: SU 463575 (on Explorer 144)
Parking: Beacon Hill car park off A34

A hilltop grave and a decorated chapel.

❶ Climb **Beacon Hill** at start or finish. Leave car park via access road. Cross **A34 bridge** to T-junction. Take footpath opposite, downhill to gate. Walk along field edge to **Old Burghclere**. Pass beside church wall and **Old Burghclere Manor** to lane. Proceed ahead, cross railway bridge and take path **L**.

❷ Keep to **L-H** field edge. Enter woodland. Shortly, bear **L** on to track bed. Turn **R**. Follow track to bridge.

❸ Bear **L** up chalky path to track. Turn **R** over bridge. Descend to lane, turn **L** then **R**, ('**Ecchinswell**'). In 50yds (46m), take waymarked bridleway **L**. Keep to path until gravel drive. Turn **L**.

❹ Follow track to **Earlstone Manor**. Proceed through or close to woodland for 1 mile (1.6km) to road. Turn **R**, then **L** along **Church Street** in Burghclere, ('**Sandham Memorial Chapel**').

❺ Turn **L** by church; keep to road, passing **Memorial Chapel** and **Carpenters Arms**, before

turning **L** along metalled dead-end lane. Pass cottage; take footpath **R** between gardens to stile. Skirt round **Budd's Farm** across 3 fields via 3 stiles; join path through trees to stile.

❻ Turn **R** along field edge, following it **L** in corner. Descend to fingerpost. Follow **L-H** path into woodland. If route is boggy, keep to field edge, looking out for gap and path **R** into woodland. Cross to stile keep ahead across field. Bear **R** through gap into field.

❼ Ignore path L. Continue, with woodland on R, to waymarker. Turn **R** towards **Ridgemoor Farm**. Pass pond to gate and track. Turn **R**, then where it bears R, turn **L** on sunken path to track. To visit **Highclere Castle**, turn **R** to road; cross **A34**; enter parkland; follow drive to house. Retrace steps and keep ahead.

❽ Turn **L** to crossroads, then **R**. Head uphill; keep to undulating track for ½ mile (800m) to Old Burghclere. Turn **L** along lane; then **R** along drive to Old Burghclere Manor. Retrace outward steps to car park.

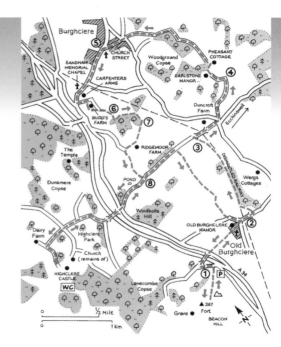

13 Minstead Church Treasures

5¼ miles (8.4km) 2hrs 30min **Ascent:** 361ft (110m)
Paths: Field paths, bridleways, forest tracks, roads, 5 stiles
Suggested map: OS Outdoor Leisure 22 New Forest
Grid reference: SU 280109 **Parking:** Minstead church or by village green

A New Forest walk starting at Minstead church – the burial place of Sir Arthur Conan Doyle.

❶ Go through gate on **R** of churchyard; walk to gate. Keep ahead; enter wood. Exit via gate. Bear **R** then **L** to road. Cross ford. Stay on lane. Go **L** by phone box.

❷ At crossroads, go straight over, following sign ('Acres Down Farm'). Cross ford; at crossroads, just past farm, turn **R**. Almost immediately take **L** fork, ('**Acres Down Car Park**'). Pass car park; follow signposts (heading for Bolderwood).

❸ Swing **R** through gate. Ignore junction R, over stream; just beyond track merging from L, turn **R** along grass track. Walk through coniferous trees, then cross gravel track and bear slightly **R**. Path swings **R**, then **L**, eventually reaching fork at top of short rise.

❹ Bear **L**, then at indistinct fork, take more distinct path **R**. Maintain direction across track; in 50yds (46m), fork **R**, vaguely parallel to track. Continue with less woodland to L; eventually exit woods via gate.

❺ Turn **R**, join track from L. Almost immediately fork **L**. With woodland to R, keep on well-defined track, ignoring routes L and R, for ½ mile (800m). Fork **R** through gorse and merge with track from R. Swing **R**, ignore track L to road, but keep ahead to reach road.

❻ Cross; walk **L** down verge. Pass **Grovewood House**; turn **L** down bridleway ('**King's Garn**'). Pass house; take **L** fork and join track merging from R. Continue downhill; just before reaching road, turn **L** over stile; continue between boundaries.

❼ Drop down to bridge and stile. Enter woodland and turn **R** through gate. Cross stream; go up steps; fork **R** through gate. Cross plank bridge, go through gate and continue gentle ascent. Join path from R and proceed into car park. Fork **R**, pass **Furzey Gardens**; walk down to road.

❽ Turn **R**, then **R** again. Take footpath **L**. Walk along **L-H** field edge to bridge and stile. Maintain direction through next field to road. Turn **R** into Minstead, then **R** after pub back to church.

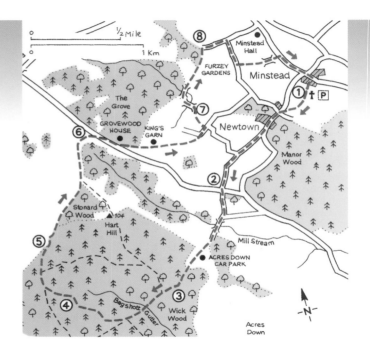

Rockbourne Roman Remains

4½ miles (7.2km) 1hr 45min **Ascent:** 295ft (90m) ⚠

Paths: Field paths, woodland bridleways and tracks, 9 stiles

Suggested map: OS Outdoor Leisure 22 New Forest or OS Explorer 130 Salisbury & Stonehenge

Grid reference: SU 113184

Parking: Rockbourne village hall car park

Roman discoveries link Rockbourne and Whitsbury, by the Wiltshire border.

❶ Turn **L** out of car park. Take lane **R** towards **Manor Farm**. Turn **R**, signed to church. Cross drive to path to **St Andrew's Church**. Keep by **R-H** edge of churchyard to junction of paths. Proceed behind houses, ignoring 2 paths R. Cross stile. Go **R** through gate.

❷ Follow field edge to junction of paths. Keep on **L** to gate. Maintain direction over 2 stiles and by field edge to stile in corner. Climb stile immediately **R**. Bear **L** by edge of meadow to stile. Pass in front of thatched cottage to stile and track, opposite **Marsh Farm**.

❸ Bear **L**, then **R** through gate. Keep to **L** through pasture to gate. Bear half **R** to gate in corner; proceed along field edge, eventually reaching stile and lane. To visit **Roman Villa**, turn **R** to T-junction, and turn **R** into entrance. Retrace steps.

❹ Take track opposite. Enter copse; at junction of tracks, take arrowed path **L** up bank into field. Keep to

L-H edge; head across field to track. Turn **R**, then **L** downhill through woodland edge. Pass house to lane.

❺ Turn **R**, then **L** along bridleway; ascend through **Radnall Wood**. At fork of paths, bear **L** (blue arrow). Pass behind **Whitsbury House** to lane. Turn **L**, then **R** along track between properties to lane. Turn **R** then **R** (by fingerpost) on bridleway through **Whitsbury Wood**.

❻ At junction with track, bear **L**; walk beside paddocks to bungalow. Turn **L** along track between paddocks towards **Whitsbury church**. Turn **L** at T-junction and shortly enter churchyard. Go through gate opposite church door to lane.

❼ Turn **L** for **Cartwheel Inn**, otherwise turn **R**, then **L** along farm drive and keep ahead, bearing **L**, then **R** between paddocks, uphill to gate. Turn **L** along field edge then head across field to track.

❽ Turn **R** and follow track **L** to junction of tracks. Cross stile opposite and walk back to Rockbourne church. Retrace steps back to village hall.

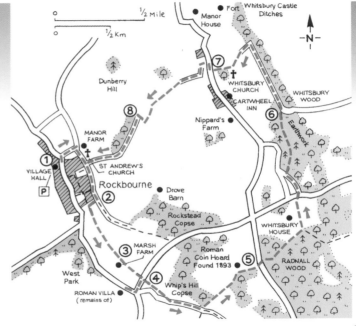

Carisbrooke's Castle A Royal Prisoner

6½ miles (10.4km) 2hrs 30min **Ascent:** 764ft (233)m **2**

Paths: Field and downland paths and tracks, some roads, 4 stiles

Suggested map: OS Outdoor Leisure 29 Isle of Wight

Grid reference: SZ 489876 **Parking:** Car park close to Carisbrooke Priory

King Charles I was imprisoned in the castle until his trial and execution in London, 1648.

❶ From car park (facing **Carisbrooke Priory**) turn **L** and walk along road. Take 1st **L-H** footpath. Shortly veer **L**, ascending through trees. On reaching **castle**, bear **L**; follow path alongside castle walls. Turn **L** towards car park; follow footpath ('**Millers Lane**').

❷ Turn **R** at road, pass **Millers Lane**; walk to stile and path on **L** ('**Bowcombe**'). Cross field to next stile; proceed across pastures, crossing several more stiles. Level with **Plaish Farm**, making for stile and junction.

❸ Bear **R**; follow enclosed path, shortly bending **L**. At **Bowcombe Farm**, turn **L**. Follow signs ('**Gatcombe**'). Pass footpath on **L**; stay on track as it curves **R**, avoiding track ahead. Veer away from track at corner of **Frogland Copse**; follow field edge to gate.

❹ Pass through trees to gate; continue up slope, skirting field boundary. Keep ahead in next field towards gate and bridleway sign. Walk along edge of **Dukem Copse**; look for turning on **L** to **Gatcombe**.

❺ Go through gate; continue along field edge. On reaching path to **Garston's**, descend to **R**; then swing **L** to gate. Follow bridleway for **Gatcombe**; turn **R** to **Newbarn Farm**. Bear **R** at entrance and, at lane, keep **R** along bridleway. At edge of **Tolt Copse** ignore path **R** and bear **L**, soon to leave **Shepherd's Trail**, proceed along bridleway towards **Sheat Manor**.

❻ Before manor, at junction of paths, turn **L**, following path past cottages. Bear **L** and keep to curving path as it ascends to woodland. Proceed through wood and down to lane by **St Olave's Church**.

❼ Turn **L** along Gatcombe Road, pass **Rectory Lane**, then turn **R** at crossing of ways, rejoining **Shepherd's Trail** for **Carisbrooke**. Pass between properties and ascend through trees. Pass over track; go through gate; follow path round **L-H** field edge.

❽ Go through gate; keep by field edge. Path later enclosed by fence and hedge to reach sign ('**Carisbrooke** and **Whitcombe Road**'). Keep to path; eventually reach junction. Continue to reach car park.

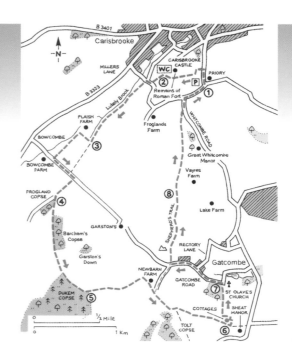

Freshwater Bay Tennyson's Island Retreat

6 miles (9.7km) 3hrs **Ascent:** 623ft (190m) ⚠️

Paths: Downland, field and woodland paths, some road walking and stretch of disused railway, 4 stiles

Suggested map: OS Outdoor Leisure 29 Isle of Wight

Grid reference: SZ 346857

Parking: Pay-and-display car park at Freshwater Bay

In the footsteps of a Romantic poet.

❶ From car park, turn **R** along road, then **L** before bus shelter along metalled track, ('Coastal Footpath'). As it bears **L**, keep ahead through kissing gates and soon begin steep ascent on concrete path on to **Tennyson Down**. Keep to well-walked path to **memorial cross** at its summit.

❷ Continue on wide grassy swathe, which narrows between gorse bushes, to reach replica of **Old Nodes Beacon**. Here, turn very sharp **R** down chalk track. At junction (car park R) keep ahead on narrow path.

❸ Path widens, then descends to gate into woodland. Proceed close to woodland fringe to further gate and enter more open countryside. Pass disused excavations on R then shortly, turn sharp **L** down unmarked path. Cross stile, then keep **L** along field boundary and bear sharp **L** to stile. Cross next field to stile and turn **R** along field edge to stile.

❹ Cross farm track, go through gate and walk along track (F47) beside **Farringford Manor Hotel**. Pass beneath wooden footbridge and continue downhill to gate and road. (Turn L to visit hotel.) Turn **R**, pass **thatched church** and turn **L** down **Blackbridge Road**. Just before Black Bridge, turn **L** into **Afton Marshes** Nature Reserve.

❺ Join nature trail, following **L-H** path beside stream to **A3055** (can be very wet in winter). Turn **L**. Almost immediately cross to join footpath F61 along old railway. In ½ mile (800m) reach the **Causeway**.

❻ Turn **R** and follow the lane to **B3399**. Turn **L** and shortly cross into unmetalled **Manor Road**. In few paces, bear off **L** ('Freshwater Way'), and ascend across grassland towards **Afton Down**.

❼ Keep ahead at junction of paths beside golf course, soon to follow gravel track **R** to clubhouse. Go through gate, pass in front of building and walk down access track, keeping **L** to **A3055**. Turn **R** downhill into **Freshwater Bay**.

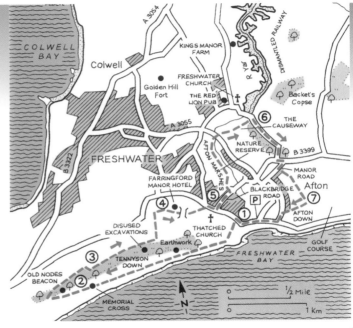

Sunningdale A Constitutional Crisis

Berkshire • Southeast England

4 miles (6.4km) 1hr 45min **Ascent:** Negligible ⚠

Paths: Enclosed woodland paths, estate drive, paths and tracks, path across golf course and polo ground; no stiles

Suggested map: OS Explorer 160 Windsor, Weybridge & Bracknell

Grid reference: SU 953676

Parking: On-street parking in Sunningdale village

Skirt the grounds of Edward VIII's favourite home, Fort Belvedere.

① From **Nags Head** turn **L**. Walk down High Street, keeping Anglican **church** on R and Baptist **church** on L. Pass Church Road and proceed along Bedford Lane. Cross brook. Turn **R** by bungalows to follow path cutting between hedgerows and fields. Look for large, shuttered house (R) just before **A30**. Bear **L**. Walk to sign on R for Shrubs Hill Lane and Onslow Road.

② Follow path to junction by panel fence. Turn **R** by bridleway/footpath sign. Make for roundabout and swing **L**, looking for footpath by house (Highgate). Follow it through woodland and when you join wider path on bend, keep **L**. Skirt **golf course**, cutting between trees and bracken. Emerge from woodland and follow path across fairways, keeping **L** at junction by bunker. Veer **L** at 1st fork, into trees, and follow path to junction with tarmac drive.

③ Turn **L** and pass through **Wentworth Estate**, cutting between exclusive houses with secluded landscaped grounds and imposing entrances. On reaching **A30**, turn **L** and follow road west. Walk down to **Berkshire/Surrey border** and bear sharp **R** to join right of way. Follow shaded woodland path between beech trees and exposed roots. Beyond wood you reach buildings of **Coworth Park**.

④ Draw level with bridge, turn **L** and then follow well-defined footpath across broad expanse of parkland, part of which is used as a **polo ground**, crossing track on far side. Enter woodland, turn **L** at road and pass several houses. When you reach speed restriction sign, bear **R** to join byway by Sunningdale **Bowling Club**. Proceed ahead on tarmac drive and continue ahead. Turn **L** at road, swinging **L** just after fork. Pass Coworth Road and return to centre of **Sunningdale**.

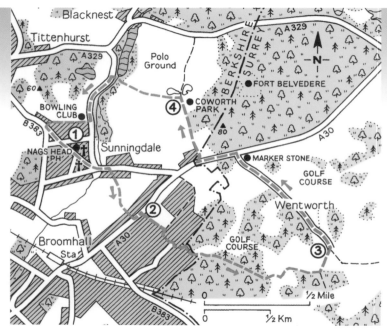

Windsor Great Park A Royal Ramble

5½ miles (8.8km) 2hrs 30min **Ascent:** 160ft (49m)
Paths: Park drives and rides, woodland paths and tracks
Suggested map: OS Explorer 160 Windsor, Weybridge & Bracknell
Grid reference: SU 947727
Parking: Car park by Cranbourne Gate

Royal footsteps on the Long Walk.

1 From car park, cross **A332** to **Cranbourne Gate** and enter park. Follow drive beside trees planted to commemorate Queen Victoria's Golden Jubilee (1887) and Edward VII's coronation (1902). Turn **R** at 1st crossroads ('**Cumberland Lodge**'); follow drive to next junction by 2 ponds.

2 Keep **L** here ('**The Village**'). Pass **Post Office** and General Store, walk between spacious green and playing field and then turn **R** to join **Queen Anne's Ride**. Look back for another view of Windsor Castle. Pass alongside **Poets Lawn** and follow ride to tarmac drive. Turn **L**; keep **L** at fork, then **L** again after a few paces at crossroads.

3 **Poets Lawn** is now on **L**. Continue ahead at next intersection; then turn **R** to follow broad, hedge-lined footpath. Ahead lies **Royal Lodge** and to **L** of it is famous **Copper Horse statue**. Take next grassy ride on **L** and head for deer gate. Keep ahead towards

statue and when you draw level with it, bear **L**. Figure of George III points the way. Follow woodland path and merge with clear track running down to drive. Pass through automatic gate and keep **R** at immediate fork.

4 Walk to **Queen Anne's Ride**, which crosses drive just before house. On **L** is millstone. Bear **R** and follow ride to **Russel's Pond**. Here, veer away from ride and keep beside pond and fence. Walk ahead between fields, making for woodland. Drop down to road at **Ranger's Gate**. Cross at lights and take tarmac drive.

5 Veer half-**L** about 100yds (91m) before some white gates and follow path across grass and alongside trees. Follow it up slope and through wood. Keep to sandy track and at point where it bends **L**, go straight on along path between trees. As it reaches gate, turn **L** and keep alongside fence. (Path can be overgrown in places.) Follow fence to drive and on **R** is outline of **Cranbourne Tower**. Bear **L** and return to car park.

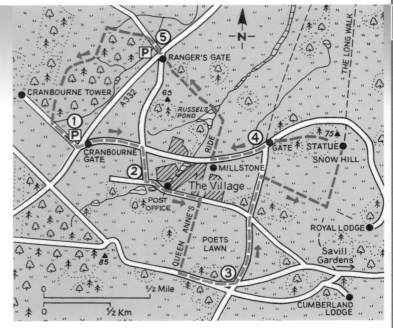

Dinton Pastures Water and Wildlife

3 miles (4.8km) 1hr 30min **Ascent:** Negligible ⓪

Paths: Lakeside and riverside paths, some road walking, no stiles

Suggested map: OS Explorer 159 Reading, Wokingham & Pangbourne

Grid reference: SU 784718

Parking: Large car park at Dinton Pastures

Enjoy this popular country park, visiting six lakes along the way.

❶ With **Tea Cosy café** and Countryside Service office on R and **High Chimneys** behind you, cross car park to large map of site. Follow wide path and keep **R** at fork ('wildlife trails'). Pass enclosed play area on L; keep Emm Brook on R.

❷ Swing **L** on reaching water; follow path alongside lake. When it veers R, turn **L** across bridge to sign ('**Tufty's Corner**'). Bear **R** here and keep **L** at fork after few paces. Follow path beside **White Swan Lake** to waymark post by patch of grass and flight of steps. Avoid steps but take **L-H** path and follow it to lake known as **Tufty's Corner**. On reaching junction by bridge, turn **R** and keep **River Loddon** on L.

❸ Walk to next bridge. Don't cross it, instead continue on riverside path. **White Swan Lake** lies over to R, glimpsed between trees. Further on, path curves to **R**, in line with river, before reaching sign

('private fishing – members only'). Join track on **R** here and bear **L**. Pass alongside Herons Water to sign ('**Sandford Lake**, **Black Swan Lake** and **Lavell's Lake** – Conservation Area'). Turn **L**; keep **Sandford Lake** on R. When path curves R, go out to road.

❹ To visit **Berkshire Museum of Aviation**, bear **L** and pass **Sandford Mill**. Take road ('No Through Road') on **L**, pass cottages and continue ahead when road dwindles to path. **Museum** is on L. Retrace route to **Sandford Mill**; keep ahead to footpath and kissing gate on **L**. Keep **L** at 1st fork, then **R** at 2nd and head for **Teal hide**. Return to road, cross over and return to lakeside path.

❺ Continue with **Sandford Lake** on R. On reaching '**Sandford Lake**' sign veer **L** over bridge and turn **L**. **Sailing Club** on L. Continue on path and look out across lake to **Goat Island**, noted for its population of goats. On reaching picnic area, turn **L** and retrace your steps back to main car park.

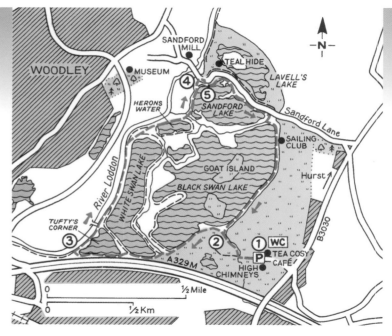

Pangbourne Fashionable Riverside Resort

3 miles (4.8km) 1hr 30min **Ascent:** Negligible ⚠

Paths: Field and riverside paths, stretches of road, section of Thames Path, 4 stiles

Suggested map: OS Explorer 159 Reading, Wokingham & Pangbourne

Grid reference: SU 633765

Parking: Car park off A329 in Pangbourne, near railway bridge

The Pang and a National Trust meadow.

❶ From car park turn **R** to mini-roundabout; walk along to church and adjoining cottage. Retrace your steps to main road, keep **Cross Keys pub** on R and turn **R** at mini-roundabout. Cross **Pang**; bear **R** at next major junction into The Moors. At end of drive continue ahead on waymarked footpath. Pass alongside various houses and patches of scrub; then go through tunnel of trees. Further on is gate with map and information board. Beyond gate **River Pang** can be seen.

❷ Follow riverside path. Make for footbridge. Don't cross it, instead, turn sharp **L** and walk across open meadow to stile in far boundary. Once over, keep alongside hedge on L and, as you approach a World War II pill box, turn **R** at path intersection and cross footbridge. Head for another footbridge on far side of field and then look for 3rd bridge with white railings, by field boundary. Cross bridge and stile beyond it; then head across field to far boundary.

❸ Exit to road and bear **L**. Follow lane between hedges and oak trees and proceed to **A329**. Go diagonally **R** to footpath by sign ('Purley Rise') and follow path north towards distant trees. Turn **R** at next bridge; follow concrete track as it bends **L** to run beneath railway line. Once through it, bear **R** to stile; then follow track along **L** edge of field, beside rivulet. Ahead on horizon are hanging woods on north bank of Thames. Pass double gates and bridge on L; continue on footpath as it crosses gentle lowland landscape. Cross stile; walk across next field to reach river bank.

❹ On reaching **River Thames**, turn **L** and head towards **Pangbourne**. Follow **Thames Path** to **Pangbourne Meadow** and up ahead now is **Whitchurch Bridge**. As you approach it, begin to veer away from river bank towards car park. Keep **L** when you get to road, pass beneath **railway line** and turn **R** at next junction. Bear **R** again at mini-roundabout and return to car park.

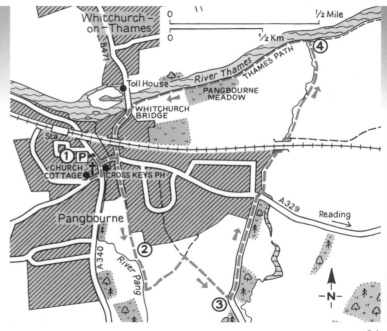

Brimpton Through Wasing Park

6 miles (9.7km) 2hrs 45min **Ascent:** 150ft (46m)

Paths: Field and woodland paths and tracks, parkland drives, meadow, road and riverside, 11 stiles

Suggested map: OS Explorer 159 Reading, Wokingham & Pangbourne

Grid reference: SU 567628

Parking: Limited spaces in lay-by opposite Pineapple pub

A walk through lovely parkland overlooking the Kennet Valley.

1 Follow path across 2 stiles to road. Cross to join byway, follow it **R** and across **common**. When it swings sharp L, keep ahead. Take path to **R** of Woodside; bear **L** at T-junction; follow path. Where it joins track, veer **L** at waymark, following field-edge path. Look for opening in trees ahead; cross bridge; turn **R** at track, following signs ('**Wasing Church**').

2 Take track, turn **L** at bend; cut through wood. Turn **R** and proceed to road. Bear **L** to junction, then **R** over **Enborne** to fork. Keep **L** and turn **R** at 'Wasing Estate' sign. Veer **L** along grassy track to junction; bear **L**.

3 Follow path to road; turn **R**, then **L** to join path. Keep to **L** edge of field, through kissing gate in top corner; veer **R**. Turn **R** to reach housing estate. Bear **R** at road; walk along to church, following path beside it. On reaching field corner, keep ahead, swinging **L** by power lines. Head south to Hyde End Lane.

4 Turn **L**, keeping **R** at fork. Look for stile to **L** of footbridge; go across meadow. Follow river bank to reach footbridge and stile. Cross over and take path to stile and bridge. Cross over road and follow track, taking path to **L** of it along woodland edge and making for bridge in far **R** corner. Follow line of trees to stile; cross next pasture towards buildings. Approaching gate and cottage veer **L** to stile. Cross to another stile by road.

5 Turn **R** over bridge; bear **L** to gate leading into Ashford Hill Meadows, veering **L** across pastures. After 75yds (68m) it becomes enclosed by trees, look for fork, and branch **L** to footbridge. Begin crossing field, after about 120yds (109m), make for gate on **L**. Swing **R** and keep **L** at fork after about 50yds (45m). Look for stile at fence corner and continue through trees. Head for stile, turn **L**. Cross over field to next stile. Proceed; when lane bends R, bear **L** and continue to road. Continue to return to lay-by.

Hermitage A Writer's Wartime Refuge

6 miles (9.7km) 2hrs 45min **Ascent:** 320ft (98m)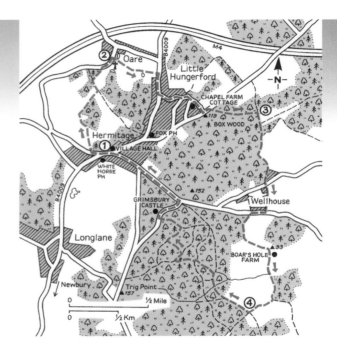

Paths: Field and woodland paths and tracks, some road, 4 stiles

Suggested map: OS Explorer 158 Newbury & Hungerford

Grid reference: SU 505730

Parking: Limited parking in Hermitage

Explore dense woodland and pass the former home of DH Lawrence on this spectacular walk near Newbury.

❶ From **village hall** in **Hermitage** turn **R**, then **R** again into Doctors Lane. Cross stile by private road sign and head across field to next stile. Pass beneath power lines and make for stile in boundary of woodland ahead. Follow footpath through trees as far as cottage. Turn **L** when you reach track and veer **R** after about 60yds (55m) at public footpath sign. Drop down through woodland to lane and keep to **R**. Walk along lane to hamlet of **Oare** and turn **R** by small pond.

❷ Head towards buildings of **Little Hungerford**, cross stile and turn **R** at road. Bear **L** into Chapel Lane and follow road round R-H bend. Pass Pond Lane and DH Lawrence's former home on corner as you head for next road junction. **Chapel Farm Cottage** is clearly identified – its front entrance is in Pond Lane and its rear garden backs on to Chapel Lane. Turn **L** and walk

along to a public footpath sign on **R**. Follow track deep into **Box Wood** and eventually reach junction.

❸ Bear **R** here and follow track through trees to next road. Cross over by bungalow and continue on next section of track. Turn **R** at next road and walk along to turning for **Boar's Hole Farm** on **L**. Follow track to farm and continue south to L-H bend. Go through gate on **R** and make for gate and house in field corner. Keep to **R** of house and turn **R** at track bend, passing through metal gate.

❹ Follow woodland track and keep **R** at fork. Go across stream and pass L turning. Take next **L** path by stream and pass over staggered junction. Turn **R** by pond, then 1st **L**, cutting through trees. Swing **R** at next junction and follow track as it runs up by seat. Keep **L** at junction and make for road by cottage. Opposite are earthworks of **Grimsbury Castle**. Turn **R** and walk along to road junction. Bear **L** and return to Hermitage.

Donnington Castle Civil War Stronghold

3 miles (4.8km) 1hr 45min **Ascent:** 165ft (50m) ▲

Paths: Paths and tracks through woods

Suggested map: OS Explorer 158 Newbury & Hungerford

Grid reference: SU 463709

Parking: Car park at Snelsmore Common Country Park

A country park and a castle.

❶ Keep toilets on R and walk ahead to barrier and country park sign. Veer **R** at fork and picnic tables and benches. Follow track to kissing gate. Beyond, track curves to **L** and then runs straight to **L** curve. Pass path on R here and continue for few paces to bridleway.

❷ Turn sharp **R** and keep **L** at next fork, avoiding path on extreme **L**. Keep to **R** of wooden seat and descend bank between bracken. Cut through trees at bottom to gate and follow path ahead as it upgrades to track. Pass **Honey Bottom Cottage** and go straight ahead when track bends R. Follow path along woodland edge until reaching wooden kissing gate on **R**.

❸ Head down field slope towards **Bagnor**, following waymarks. Make for gate and follow grassy path to road. Turn **L**, pass **Blackbird Inn** and follow track at end of car park. Go through kissing gate and take tarmac path over **A34** to golf course. Keep **L** at fork on far side of footbridge, heading towards woodland and

intersection. Cross drive and follow waymarked path on **R**, threading through trees. Keep greens and fairways on R. Emerge from woodland at gate and climb slope to **Donnington Castle**.

❹ Look for gate behind it, leading to track. Turn **L**. Pass between barns of **Castle Farm**. Bear **L** down tarmac bridleway. Re-cross bypass and sweep **R**, following drive as it dwindles to track. Keep **R** at fork and cut between fences. On L are extensive fairways. Follow track towards house and keep to **L** of it.

❺ Pass through gate on to **Snelsmore Common** and keep ahead at waymarked junction. Pass beneath power lines and continue between bracken and gorse bushes. Keep **R** at next fork and follow waymark pointing towards car park. A useful landmark is fire control tower. Merge with another path at next waymark and, within sight of road and just before stile, look for gate on your **L**. Go through it and return to car park.

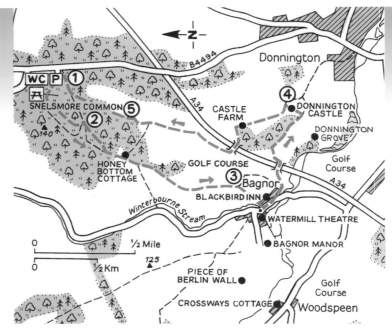

Farnborough The Old Rectory

7½ miles (12.1km) 3hrs **Ascent:** 150ft (46m)

Paths: Bridleways, field paths, tracks and quiet lanes, no stiles

Suggested map: OS Explorer 170 Abingdon & Wantage

Grid reference: SU 471825

Parking: Room to park in West Ilsley's main street

To the former home of a poet, John Betjeman.
1 Follow road out of **West Ilsley**, heading west. Take 1st bridleway on **L** and make for gate. Continue ahead with field boundary on R. Bear **L** at next junction, and then almost immediately **R** to follow path across large field. Look for boundary corner ahead and keep ahead in next field, with fence on R. Follow path across field to road by **Upper Farm**, veer **L** and walk along to **Farnborough church** and **Old Rectory**.
2 Walk along road to farm, rejoin track beside outbuildings and look for waymark and galvanised gates after about 60yds (55m). Field footpath and 2 tracks can be seen here. Keep **R**, alongside farm. Cut between trees, bushes and margins of vegetation and cross track further on. Continue ahead to junction with byway and bridleway. Keep going through woodland, following Ilsley Downs Riding Route. Make for next junction, where you can see field beyond the trees, bear **R** and follow clear path through woods.

3 Keep **R** at road and when it bends R, keep ahead along bridleway running across fields towards trees. At length, bridleway becomes byway. Keep ahead on reaching bend and walk along to on **L**. Take it into woodland and down slope. As you approach gap in hedge, with field ahead, veer **R** to follow path running through trees. Eventually it climbs gently to junction. Walk turns **L**, but it is worth stepping to R for several paces to admire timeless view of **Woolvers Barn** and Woolvers Down.
4 Follow byway, avoiding public footpath on R, and take next bridleway on **L**. Keep **R** at next junction and cut between hedges. When track bends **L**, there is memorable view of **West Ilsley** sitting snug in its downland setting. Keep **R** at next junction, following track alongside **West Ilsley Stables**. Walk down to and turn **L**. As it bends R by bridleway sign, go straight on by **Keeper's Stables**. Swing **L** as you reach centre of **West Ilsley** and pass **All Saints Church**.

Stowe Majestic Paradise

4½ miles (7.2km) 2hrs **Ascent:** Negligible

Paths: Field paths, estate drives, stretches of road, 5 stiles

Suggested map: OS Explorer 192 Buckingham & Milton Keynes

Grid reference: SP 684357

Parking: On-street parking in Chackmore

Savour the delights of Stowe, with its famous 18th-century landscape garden.

❶ Walk through **Chackmore**, pass **Queens Head** and continue through village. At speed derestriction signs, keep ahead for few paces and look for path on **L**. Aim diagonally **R** in field, passing under power lines. Make for stile beneath branches of oak in corner where waymarks indicate that path forks.

❷ Cross field towards 2 stiles, making for one on **L**, beyond which is plank bridge. Keep to **R** boundary of elongated field and when it widens, go diagonally **R** to far corner. **Stowe Castle** is visible to R and outline of **Corinthian Arch** to L. Join track, pass under telegraph wires and look for gap and waymark as track curves **R** by hedge corner. Veer over to **R** in field and look for path ('Farey Oak'). Avoid this route and make for footbridge and stile few paces away.

❸ Cross into field and head up slope, keeping to **L** of 2 distant houses. Head for single-storey dwelling in top corner and as you climb slope, outline of **Gothic Temple** looms into view. Go through gate at **Lamport** and continue ahead on bridleway. The **Bourbon Tower** is clearly visible. Pass through gate and keep ahead towards monument commemorating Duke of Buckingham. Merge with another path and keep sports ground on R.

❹ Make for gate leading out to avenue of trees running down towards **Grecian Valley**. Cross over and follow grass track up to clump of trees. Bear **L** here and follow avenue (part of **Roman road**). Pass magnificent façade of **Stowe School** and keep along main drive. On reaching **Boycott Pavilions**, branch off half-**L** at stile and sign for **Corinthian Arch**. Down below lies **Oxford Water**, crossed by stone bridge.

❺ Follow drive through parkland. Drive eventually reaches **Corinthian Arch**. Line up with arch and enjoy views of **Stowe School**. Walk down avenue to road junction, swing **L** and return to **Chackmore**.

The Claydons Lady with the Lamp

5½ miles (8.8km) 2hrs Ascent: 160ft (49m) ⚠

Paths:	Field paths and tracks, several stretches of road
Suggested map:	OS Explorer 192 Buckingham & Milton Keynes
Grid reference:	SP 739255
Parking:	On-street parking in road leading to St Mary the Virgin Church, East Claydon

Visit a National Trust house and the bedroom occupied by Florence Nightingale.

❶ Walk along Church Way into village centre. Keep **R** at next junction, following **Sandhill Road**. Pass houses and swing **L** through gate, before brick and timber cottage. Keep ahead towards next gate; look for gate and waymark few paces to **L** of it. Keep ahead in field, with boundary on **R**. Make for gate in corner and cross to boundary. Continue ahead with hedgerow on **L**, following track along field perimeter, towards **Home Farm**. Look for plank bridge and stile to **L** of track; cross cemetery to stile by road.

❷ Bear **L**. Follow road for 600yds (549m). Pass entrance to **Home Farm** (R) and footpath (L). Turn **L**. Follow drive to **Claydon House**. At cattle grid just in front of it, bear **R** through 2 gates then **L**. Keeping **Claydon House** and **church** L, continue beside ha-ha, with lake to R. Cut through parkland to gate, merge with drive to **Claydon House** and follow to road.

❸ Turn **R** and pass lay-by. Keep ahead to stile in L boundary. Head diagonally **L** towards hedge corner, making for stile close to it. Maintain direction and make for extreme **L** corner of **Home Wood**. Cross 2nd stile and look for 3rd stile by woodland edge. Keep telegraph wires (L) and look for waymark in corner. Cross stile, keeping to **L** of hedge. Make for gate and stile ahead. Cross tarmac drive to **Muxwell Farm**.

❹ Beyond gate, head diagonally **L** and look for waymark in line of trees across pasture. Veer **R** in next field, making for stile and post in boundary. Walk diagonally **R** across field to far corner, pass through gap and keep to **R** edge of pasture. Bear **R** at gateway to track and turn **L**. Walk along to road and turn **R**.

❺ Walk through **Botolph Claydon**. Bear **L** at junction, following signs, ('**East Claydon** and **Winslow**'). Pass Botolph Farmhouse, **library** and hall. Follow pavement to sign ('footpath only, no horses'). Take path back to **East Claydon**.

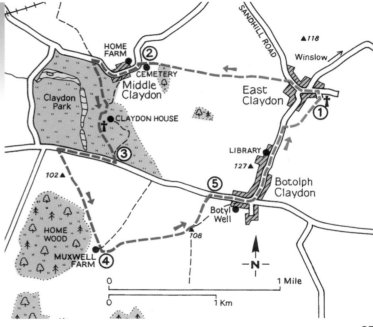

27 Mentmore Crime of the Century

6½ miles (10.4km) 2hrs 45min **Ascent:** 180ft (55m)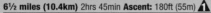

Paths: Field paths and tracks, roads and canal tow path, 2 stiles
Suggested map: OS Explorers 181 Chiltern Hills North; 192 Milton Keynes & Buckingham
Grid reference: Grid reference: SP 907196 (on Explorer 181)
Parking: Limited parking in vicinity of Stag pub at Mentmore

Enjoy an amble in the Vale of Aylesbury, passing the site of the Great Train Robbery.

❶ Walk back to junction by **Stag**, turn **R** and pass one of **Mentmore Towers'** entrances. Follow road round to **L**, then **R** by Church of St Mary the Virgin. Continue along road; bear **R** at stile, just beyond **Vicarage Cottage**. Go down field, keeping fence to R; look for stile in bottom boundary.

❷ Veer **R** briefly to plank bridge; swing **L** to skirt field, keeping ditch on R. On reaching next plank bridge and waymark, look for pond. Follow path alongside it into next field and pass under telegraph wires to next plank bridge in boundary. Keep ahead and pass under electricity cables. Houses of **Ledburn** can be seen ahead. Make for footbridge; in next field aim slightly **L**, towards house. Keep to L of it, turning **R** at road.

❸ Walk through **Ledburn**, making for **L** bend. On **L** is **Cornfield Cottage**. Cross road to kissing gate and follow track running across farmland. As it curves L,

keep ahead, following path across field. On reaching track, turn **R** and follow it to **Sears Crossing**. Cross **railway bridge**, follow track down to road. Turn **L**.

❹ Bear **R** at sign for Grove Church and Farm and down to **Grand Union Canal** at **Church Lock**. Pass Church Lock Cottage before turning **R** to join tow path. Follow **Grand Union** for about 1 mile (1.6km) and, about 140yds (128m) before bridge, with **weir** on the L, leave tow path at plank bridge and bear **R** for few paces to field corner.

❺ Swing **L** and keep boundary on R. Make for 2 gates leading out to road, turn **R**, then **L** at turning for Wing and **Ledburn**. Follow road to **Bridego Bridge**, pass beneath **railway**; keep ahead to **Rowden Farm**.

❻ Bear **L** at next junction for **Mentmore**. Pass Mentmore Courts and **Stud House** before turning **L** at end of stretch of pavement. Opposite junction are 2 wooden gates leading into field. Follow road round to **R** and return to playground and parking area.

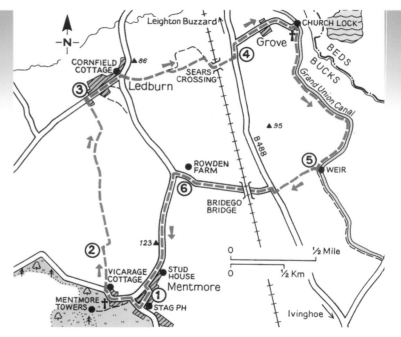

Hartwell A Green Abode

5 miles (8km) 2hrs **Ascent:** 180ft (55m) ⚠️

Paths: Field and riverside paths, tracks and lanes, 6 stiles

Suggested map: OS Explorer 181 Chiltern Hills North

Grid reference: SP 783123

Parking: Space in Eythrope Road, Hartwell

By the River Thame and through the grounds of Hartwell House.

1 From **A418** turn into Bishopstone Road and keep to **L** of church. Walk along to footpath beside Manor Farm Close and cross pasture to kissing gate leading out to recreation ground. Pass ornate gate pillars on **L**, recalling village men who died in world wars. Exit to road by railings. Cross over to footpath sign and gate for Woodspeen and follow drive to timber garage and shed. Bear **R** to gate and follow path to road. Turn **R**, walk up to **A418**. **Rose and Crown** is on **R**.

2 Swing **L** at corner. Follow path beside stone wall. Head for road, bear **R** and walk to **Hartwell House** entrance. Veer **L** at gate pillars. Follow waymarked path through hotel grounds. Go through kissing gate, keep church **R** and graveyard **L**. Turn **R** at road and pass pavilion. Avoid **North Bucks Way** to **L**, pass **Lower Hartwell Farm**. Turn **L** at footpath. Cross 2 fields via 3 stiles. Turn **R** just beyond plank bridge.

3 Skirt field, making for stile ahead. Keep hedge on **L** and continue on **North Bucks Way**, heading towards **Waddon Hill Farm**. Cross stile, walk ahead alongside timber barns; turn **L** at waymark. Follow track across fields. When it eventually sweeps **L**, leave it and go proceed along a path to stile. Cross meadow and head for **River Thame**. Swing **L** at river bank to gate and join **Thame Valley Walk**.

4 After about 60yds (55m) path reaches 2nd gate, where river begins wide loop away to **R**. Follow stream to next gate and rejoin river bank. Follow **Thame**, avoiding bridleway branching away from river, and continue on waymarked trail. Make for footbridge and weir, on opposite bank is ornate **lodge**. Join concrete track and follow it towards trees.

5 Once in trees, river is on **L** and **Eythrope Park** is on **R**. Bear **R** at next junction. To continue, keep **L** and follow tarmac drive. Begin moderate lengthy ascent before reaching **Stone**.

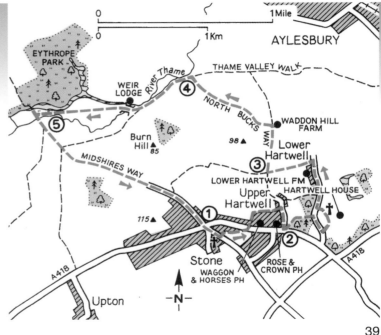

Jordans Water of Peace

6¾ miles (10.9km) 2hrs 45min **Ascent:** 98ft (30m)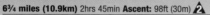

Paths: Paths across farmland and some road walking, 12 stiles

Suggested map: OS Explorer 172 Chiltern Hills East

Grid reference: SU 991937

Parking: Car park off main street, almost opposite church

Visit a Quaker settlement and museum recalling the life of poet William Penn.

❶ From car park turn **R** and walk through village. After ¾ mile (1.2km), bear **R** into Back Lane, shortly swinging **L**. Keep **L** at fork, avoid stile in boundary; continue to wide gap in hedge, just before field corner. Cross into adjoining field and proceed in same direction, following path for about 60yds (55m) to stile. Keep ahead in next field, with hedge on **L**, heading for stile. Follow path across fields and between trees until reaching stile and waymark.

❷ Turn **L**; skirt field to gate and stile. Path runs through trees to next stile and drive beyond. Follow it by **New Barn Farm** to road. Turn **L** and **L** again at junction. Bear **R** just beyond **L** bend. Follow waymarked track to Willow Court Stables. Go through kissing gate. Follow path by paddocks.

❸ At path crossroads, turn **R**. Go through kissing gate, under power cables. Make for stile and gate; cross recreation ground. Keep ahead, cross drive to **Manor Farm**. Follow tree-lined path. Head for path junction; proceed between houses. Cross Copse Lane. Follow Seer Green Lane into village. Continue to junction. Turn **R** towards **Seer Green**. Pass **Old Jordans Guest House**; follow road to **Meeting House**.

❹ Turn **L** into **Welders Lane**; pass **youth hostel**. Continue along lane to track on **L**, ('Grove Farm'). Keep ahead to stile on **L**, just before private property sign. Head diagonally across paddock, passing under power cables. Cross 4 stiles. Turn **R** and follow fenced path to gate. Keep along woodland edge, pass path on **R** and continue to junction by corner of wire fence.

❺ Swing **R**; go through trees to stile by road. Cross; follow enclosed path. Eventually reach track by bungalow, '**Brymavic**'. Cross and continue on path as it skirts bowling green, playing fields and recreation ground. Look for path in corner and keep to **R** of a **school**. Go down to road, turn **R** to return to car park.

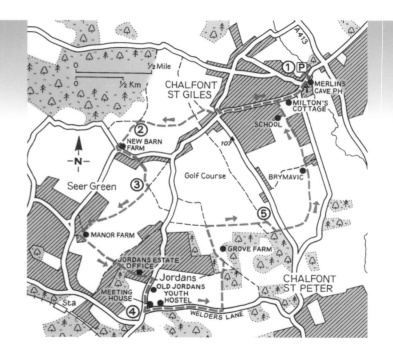

West Wycombe Disraeli's Des Res

7 miles (11.3km) 2hrs 45min **Ascent:** 280ft (85m)

Paths: Field, woodland and parkland paths, some roads, 5 stiles

Suggested map: OS Explorer 172 Chiltern Hills East

Grid reference: SU 826952

Parking: Car park by church and mausoleum at West Wycombe

Visit Hughenden Manor, home of famous British statesman Benjamin Disraeli.

❶ From car park pass to immediate **R** of **church**. Continue to **mausoleum** and line up with **A40** below. Take grassy path down hillside, avoiding path on R and walk to fork. Keep **R** to steps; descend to road. Bear **L** and pass Church Lane on R. Take next path on **R**; keeping to field **R-H** boundary. Look for stile and maintain same direction to stile by road.

❷ Cross over, making for gate; pass under **railway**. At field keep ahead keeping **R** of fence. Follow path to stile; cross track and continue up slope. Make for 2 stiles by gate and barns. Join lane, swing **R** at waymark and follow ride through woodland. Eventually reach a stile with path crossing field beyond.

❸ On reaching track, turn **R** and cut through wood. Veer **L** at fork and head for road. Bear **L** into **Downley**. Turn L for **pub** or **R** to continue. Pass houses; when track bends L, keep ahead briefly, veering **L** at waymark. Cross common, following path through clearings and into trees. At National Trust sign, turn sharp **L** and follow path through woods. Avoid path on L following white arrows. Pass gate and continue ahead, up moderately steep slope to junction.

❹ Keep **R**; follow path to track. Swing **L** to visit **Hughenden Manor** or **R** to continue. Follow path through parkland, making for trees. Bear immediately **L**, up slope. Look for house; turn **R** at road. Pass **Bricklayers Arms** and straight ahead at junction.

❺ Keep ahead through trees to housing estate. Go forward for several paces at road, bearing **R** at 1st footpath sign. Follow path as it bends **L** and leads to junction. Swing **L** for several steps; veer **R** by houses, heading through trees to galvanised gate. Take sunken path to **R** of gate, follow it to fork and continue ahead. Head for lane and follow it towards **West Wycombe**. Cross **Bradenham Road**; proceed into village. Turn **R** into West Wycombe Hill Road. Head uphill to car park.

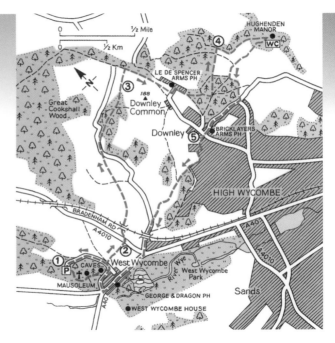

Turville The Rolling Chilterns

3 miles (4.8km) 1hr 30min **Ascent:** 150ft (45m)

Paths: Field and woodland paths, some road walking, 9 stiles
Suggested map: OS Explorer 171 Chiltern Hills West
Grid reference: SU 767911
Parking: Small parking area in centre of Turville

Enjoy views, made famous by film.

1 The walk starts from **Turville**, one of Britain's most frequently used film and television locations, including *Chitty Chitty Bang Bang*, *The New Avengers* and *The Vicar of Dibley*. Take lane just to **L** of church entrance, with Sleepy Cottage on corner. Pass Square Close Cottages and school before continuing on Chiltern Way through trees. Climb to gate. Keep ahead along field edge to waymark in boundary. Branch half-**L** at this point, heading diagonally down field to stile.

2 Cross road to further stile. Follow track through trees, passing gas installation on R. Pass bench on L before exiting trees. Avoid path branching off to R and continue up field slope to next belt of trees. **Turville** is clearly seen over to L. Enter woodland; at junction keep **L**. Follow clear wide path as it contours round slopes. Descend hillside, keeping to woodland edge. Follow fence and bear **L** at next corner, heading to stile by **Poynatts Farm**.

3 Walk along drive to road; bear **R** and enter Skirmett. On R is **Cobs Cottage** and next door is Ramblers. Pass **The Frog Inn** and follow road south to next junction. Houses, telephone box and post box line route. Turn **L**, pass stile on R and walk along to next **L** footpath. Follow field edge to bungalow and stile, cross over to drive and make for road.

4 Bear **R**, heading out of village, to junction with Watery Lane. Signs ('Except for access') can be seen now. Look for stile and footpath immediately to **R** of it. Cross field to stile in corner and make for boundary hedge ahead in next field. Cross stile and head diagonally **R** to hedge by houses. Once over stile, take road opposite ('Ibstone and Stokenchurch').

5 Walk up road for about 120yds (110m) and swing **L** at 1st waymarked junction. Follow Chiltern Way between trees, offering glimpses of Chilterns. Cross stile and head diagonally down field towards **Turville**. Make for track; follow it to village green.

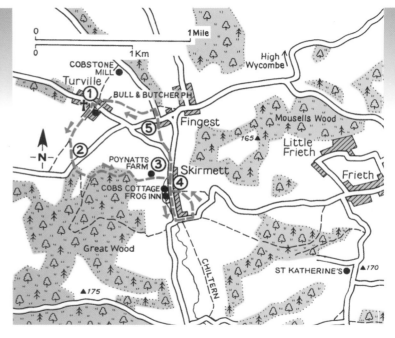

Burnham Beeches Space in a Bustling World

4½ miles (7.2km) 1hr 45min **Ascent:** 150ft (46m) ⚠

Paths: Woodland paths and drives, field paths, tracks and stretches of road, 9 stiles

Suggested map: OS Explorer 172 Chiltern Hills East

Grid reference: SU 957850

Parking: Car park at Burnham Beeches

Enjoy the spacious clearings and sunny glades of a National Nature Reserve.

❶ Follow drive away from **Farnham Common**, keeping car parking area on your L. Pass refreshment kiosk and veer **R** at fork just beyond. Soon reach gate where you enter National Nature Reserve's car-free zone. Follow **Halse Drive** as it curves **L** and down between trees. When you reach bottom of hill swing **L** into **Victoria Drive**.

❷ Follow broad stony drive between beeches, avoiding turnings either side of route; eventually reach major junction with wide path on L and R. On R is large beech tree with 'Andy 6.9.97' carved on trunk. If you miss path, you shortly reach road. Bear **R** and go up slope, keep **L** at fork and cross several clearings to reach road at junction with Green Lane and **Park Lane**.

❸ Cross road to stile and waymark and go straight ahead, keeping boundary on L. Make for stile and descend into field dip, quickly climbing again to pass

alongside grounds of **Dorney Wood**. Walk ahead to field corner, cross stile and turn **R** at road. Head for waymarked footpath on **L** and cross field to gap in trees and hedgerow. Turn **R** and skirt fields, making for belt of trees and banks of undergrowth. Path cuts between 2 oak trees in next field before reaching gap in hedgerow.

❹ Cross stile out to road; turn **L**. Pass Common Lane and Horseshoe Hill; turn **R** at next bridleway. Follow track through wood to next road at **Littleworth Common**. Cross stile to **R** of **Blackwood Arms** and follow Beeches Way. Beyond next stile continue ahead alongside wood, crossing 2 stiles before following fenced path. Go through gate and take path between trees of **Dorney Wood**.

❺ On reaching stile, cross over to road and continue on Beeches Way. Make for next major intersection and keep **R** along **Halse Drive**. Pass **Victoria Drive** and retrace your steps back to car park.

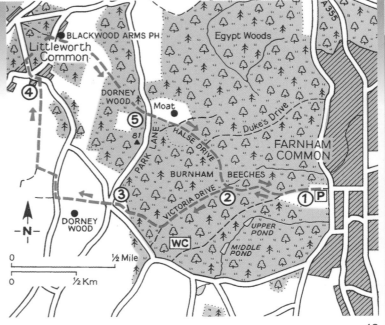

33

Dorney Medieval Village Manor House

5 miles (8km) 1hrs 45min **Ascent:** Negligible ⓘ

Paths: Roads, firm paths and Thames tow path

Suggested map: OS Explorer 160 Windsor, Weybridge & Bracknell

Grid reference: SU 938776

Parking: Large car park at Dorney Common

Buckinghamshire • Southeast England

Take a stroll by the Thames and visit Dorney Court – unchanged for 600 years.

❶ From car park follow road across **Dorney Common**, towards **Dorney** village. Pass Wakehams, a timber-framed house with a well, and away to R is a fine view of Windsor Castle. Keep **L** at T-junction, cross cattle grid and join pavement. Walk through **Dorney**, keeping **Palmer Arms** on your R. Bear **L** into Court Lane and pass entrance to **Dorney Court**. Follow path parallel to road; shortly reach **Church of St James the Less**.

❷ Continue on path and when road bends R, keep ahead at sign for Dorney Lake, Park and Nature Reserve. Keep to **R-H** side of drive and follow parallel path as it sweeps away to **R** by plaque and grove of trees. Further on path passes over conveyor belt carrying sand and gravel from nearby quarry works. Make for some trees and reach Thames Path by Sustrans waymark.

❸ Turn **L**. Follow national trail, keeping **Bray Marina** on opposite bank. Further downstream the imposing cream façade of **Bray film studios** edges into your view. Continue on leafy Thames Path and soon you will catch sight of **Oakley Court** across water on Berkshire bank.

❹ Beyond hotel can be seen cabin cruisers and gin palaces of **Windsor Marina** and next to it lines of caravans and mobile homes. Through trees on Buckinghamshire bank is outline of Eton College's new boathouse and rowing lake. To gain closer view, briefly follow path beside river boathouse and slipway, walk towards lake and then retrace your steps to Thames Path. On opposite bank is Windsor Race Course Yacht Basin and ahead is **Chapel of St Mary Magdalen**. Follow path alongside **chapel** to kissing gate and about 50yds (46m) beyond it reach lane. With Old Place opposite and avenue of chestnut trees on R, turn **L** and return to car park.

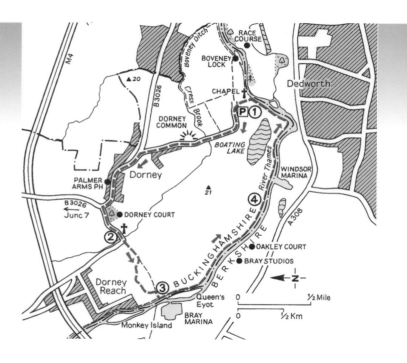

Devil's Dyke A Grand View

3 miles (4.8km) 1hr 30min Ascent: 656ft (200m) △

Paths: Field and woodland paths, 6 stiles
Suggested map: OS Explorer 122 South Downs Way – Steyning to Newhaven
Grid reference: TQ 268112
Parking: Summer Down free car park

A fine walk with glimpses over the most famous of all the dry chalk valleys, the South Downs.

❶ From **Summer Down** car park go through kissing gate and veer **R**. Join **South Downs Way** and follow it alongside lines of trees. Soon path curves **L** and then drops down to road. Leave **South Downs Way** here, as it crosses over to join private road to **Saddlescombe**, and follow verge for about 75yds (68m). Bear **L** at footpath sign and drop down bank to stile.

❷ Follow line of tarmac lane as it curves **R** to reach waymark. Leave lane and walk ahead alongside power lines, keeping line of trees and bushes on **R**. Look for narrow path disappearing into vegetation and make for stile. Descend steps into woods and turn **R** at junction with bridleway. Take path running off half-**L** and follow it between fields and wooded dell. Pass over stile and continue to stile in **L** boundary. Cross footbridge to further stile; now turn **R** towards **Poynings**.

❸ Head for gate and footpath sign and turn **L** at road. Follow parallel path along to **Royal Oak**; then continue to **Dyke Lane** on **L**. There is **memorial stone** here, dedicated to George Stephen Cave Cuttress, a Poynings resident for over 50 years, and erected by his widow. Follow tarmac bridleway and soon it narrows to path. On reaching fork, by National Trust sign for **Devil's Dyke**, veer **R** and begin climbing steps.

❹ Follow path up to gate and continue up stairs. From higher ground there are breathtaking views to north and west. Make for kissing gate and head up slope towards inn. Keep **Devil's Dyke pub** on **L** and take road round to **L**, passing bridleway on **L**. Follow path parallel to road and look to **L** for definitive view of **Devil's Dyke**.

❺ Head for **South Downs Way** and turn **L** by National Trust sign for **Summer Down** to stile and gate. Follow trail, keeping **Devil's Dyke** down to **L**, and eventually reaching stile leading into **Summer Down car park**.

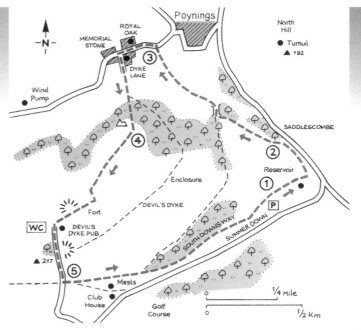

Climping Countryside Meets Coast

4 miles (6.4km) 2hrs **Ascent:** Negligible

Paths: Field paths, roads and stretches of beach, 1 stile

Suggested map: OS Explorer 121 Arundel & Pulborough

Grid reference: TQ 005007

Parking: Car park at Climping Beach

An invigorating walk on the last surviving stretch of undeveloped coast between Bognor Regis and Brighton.

1 From beach car park take road heading away from sea, passing entrance to **Bailiffscourt Hotel** on L-H side. Continue walking along road until you reach **The Black Horse pub** and then take next footpath on **R**, by thatched cottages.

2 When track swings **L**, continue walking ahead across field to junction with byway. Go straight over and follow path through fields, heading for derelict outbuildings.

3 Join track on bend and turn **R**. As it swings R, take signposted path; begin by following boundary hedge. Stride across field, cross concrete footbridge and bear **L** at footpath sign to follow deep ditch known as **Ryebank Rife**. When path veers away from ditch, cross field to line of trees. There is stile here, followed by footbridge.

4 Turn **R** and walk along road to turning on **R** for **Littlehampton Golf Club**. Route follows this road but before taking it, continue ahead briefly, to look at footbridge crossing Arun. Buildings of Littlehampton can be seen on far side and you may like to extend walk by visiting town.

5 Continuing main walk, follow road towards **West Beach** and **golf club**, veering **R** at car park sign. Follow enclosed path to kissing gate and briefly cross golf course to enter wood. Greens and fairways are visible as you pick your way between trees. Keep to path; eventually reach house, 'The Mill'. Avoid path on R here and keep **L**.

6 Continue on footpath and soon it reaches **West Beach**. Look for interpretation board, which explains how this stretch of coastline has been shaped and influenced by climatic conditions and the sea. Follow footpath sign towards **Climping**, skirting beach and avoiding byway on R as you approach beach car park.

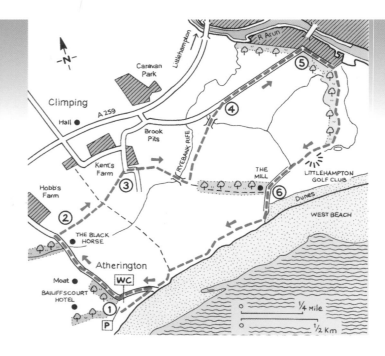

Arundel Sussex Stronghold

3¼ miles (5.3km) 2hrs **Ascent:** 197ft (60m)

Paths: Riverside and parkland paths, some road walking, 2 stiles

Suggested map: OS Explorer 121 Arundel & Pulborough

Grid reference: TQ 020071

Parking: Mill Road fee-paying car park, Arundel **Note:** Arundel Park is closed annually on 24th March

Along the River Arun to Arundel Park.

1 From car park in **Mill Road** turn **R** and walk along tree-lined pavement. Pass **bowling green** – glance to L reveals dramatic view of historic **Arundel Castle** with its imposing battlements. There has been a castle here since the 11th century, though most of the present fortification is Victorian. Arundel Castle is the principal ancestral home of the Dukes of Norfolk. The castle was attacked by parliamentary forces during the Civil War but was extensively rebuilt and restored in the 18th and 19th centuries.

2 Follow road to stone bridge, cross over via footbridge and turn **R** to join riverside path. Emerging from cover, path cuts across lush, low-lying ground to reach western bank of **Arun**. Turn **L** and walk beside reed-fringed **Arun** to **Black Rabbit pub**, which stands out against curtain of trees.

3 From **Black Rabbit**, follow minor road in roughly westerly direction back towards **Arundel**, passing entrance to **Wildfowl and Wetlands Trust**. Make for gate leading into Arundel Park and follow path alongside **Swanbourne Lake**. Eventually lake fades from view as walk reaches deeper into park. Ignore turning branching off to **L**, just before gate and stile, and follow path as it curves gently to **R**.

4 Turn sharply to **L** at next waymarked junction and begin fairly steep ascent, with footpath through park seen curving away down to L, back towards lake. This stretch of walk offers fine views over Arundel Park. Head for a stile and gate then bear immediately **R** up bank. Cross grass, following waymarks and keeping to **L** of **Hiorne Tower**. On reaching driveway, turn **L** and walk down to Park Lodge. Keep to **R** by private drive and make for road.

5 Turn **L**, pass **Arundel Cathedral** and bear **L** at road junction by entrance to **Arundel Castle**. Go down hill, back into centre of **Arundel**. You'll find **Mill Road** at bottom of High Street.

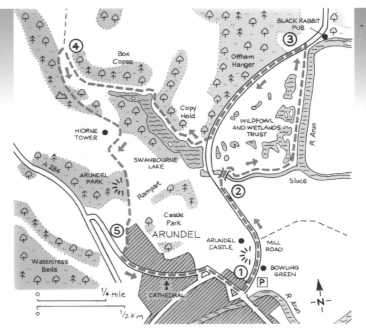

Slindon Treasures in Trust

West Sussex • Southeast England

4 miles (6.4km) 2hrs **Ascent:** 82ft (25m) ▲

Paths: Woodland, downland paths and tracks, 4 stiles
Suggested map: OS Explorer 121 Arundel & Pulborough
Grid reference: SU 960076
Parking: Free National Trust car park in Park Lane, Slindon

Tour and explore a sprawling National Trust estate on this glorious woodland walk.

❶ From car park walk down towards road and turn **R** at sign ('No riding') passing through gate to join wide, straight path cutting between trees and bracken. Path runs alongside sunny glades and clearings and between lines of beech and silver birch trees before reaching crossroads.

❷ Turn **R** to 2nd crossroads and continue ahead here, keeping grassy mound and ditch, all remains of **Park Pale**, on R. Follow broad path as it begins wide curve to **R**; boundary ditch is still visible here, running keep ahead, soon skirting fields. As you approach entrance to **Slindon campsite**, swing **L** and follow track down to road.

❸ Turn **L** and follow road through woodland. Pass **Slindon Bottom Road** and turn **R** after few paces to join bridleway. Follow path as it cuts between fields and look for path on **R**.

❹ Cross stile, go down field and up other side to next stile to join track. Turn **R**. Follow this track as it bends **L**. Walk along to **Row's Barn**, cross stile and continue on track. **Nore Folly** can be seen over to L.

❺ Continue ahead on track, following it to double gates and stile. Pass to R of **Courthill Farm**, turn **R** and follow lane or parallel woodland path to next road. Bear **L** and pass **Slindon College** and **St Richard's Catholic Church** on R before reaching **Church Hill**.

❻ To visit **Newburgh Arms**, continue ahead along Top Road. Otherwise, follow **Church Hill**, pass church and make for **pond**. Look for mallard ducks here. Follow obvious waterside path to enter woodland. At fork, by National Trust sign for **Slindon Estate**, keep **L** and walk through trees to car park. To celebrate its centenary in 1995, the National Trust chose the **Slindon Estate** to launch its 100 Paths Project, which offers many miles of footpaths and bridleways – just perfect for country walking.

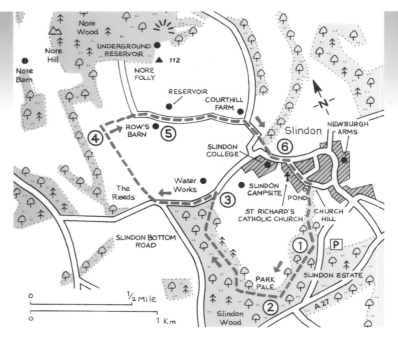

Goodwood Glorious Good Going

3½ miles (5.7km) 1hr 30min **Ascent:** 328ft (100m) ▲

Paths: Woodland tracks and field paths, section of Monarch's Way and one lengthy stretch of quiet road, 4 stiles

Suggested map: OS Explorers 120 Chichester, South Harting & Selsey; 121 Arundel & Pulborough

Grid reference: TQ 897113 (on Explorer 120)

Parking: Counter's Gate free car park and picnic area at Goodwood Country Park or large free car park opposite racecourse

A lovely woodland walk beside one of Britain's best-known racecourses.

❶ Make for western end of **Counter's Gate** car park and look for footpath sign by opening leading out to road. Cross over to junction of 2 clear tracks, with path on R. Follow R-H track ('public footpath'), which is part of **Monarch's Way**, to gate and stile. Continue to next gate and stile then cross clearing in woods.

❷ Cut through remote, thickly wooded country, following gently curving path over grassland and down between trees to reach gateway. Village of **East Dean** can be seen nestling down below. Head diagonally R down steep field slope to stile in corner.

❸ Cross into adjacent field and follow boundary to 2nd stile leading out to road. Bear L and walk down into **East Dean**, passing **Manor Farm**. Keep R at junction in village centre and, if it's opening time,

follow road towards Petworth in order to visit **Hurdlemakers Inn**.

❹ Leave **East Dean** by keeping pond on R-H side and follow road towards neighbouring **Charlton**. On reaching village, pass **Fox Goes Free** pub and **Woodstock House Hotel** and take next L turning. Follow lane to stile on R and turning on L. To visit **Open Air Museum** at Singleton, cross over into fields and follow straight path. Return to this stile by same route and take road opposite.

❺ Walk along to junction and turn R by war memorial, dedicated to fallen comrades of Sussex Yeomanry in both World Wars. Follow **Chalk Road**, which dwindles to track on outskirts of **Charlton**. Once clear of village, track climbs steadily between trees. Follow track eventually to reach road and cross over to **Counter's Gate** car park.

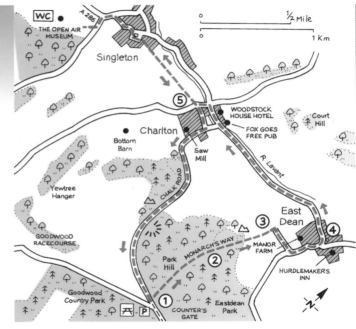

Midhurst Town and Country

3 miles (4.8km) **2hrs** **Ascent:** 123ft (37m)

Paths: Pavements, field, riverside tracks and country road, 4 stiles
Suggested map: OS Explorer 120 Chichester, South Harting & Selsey
Grid reference: SZ 886217
Parking: Car park by tourist information centre in North Street

Follow the River Rother to the ruins of Cowdray House.

❶ From car park by tourist information centre turn **L** and walk along **North Street**, passing post office. Bear **L** into **Knockhundred Row** ('South Pond'). Walk along **Church Hill** and into South Street, passing historic **Spread Eagle Hotel**.

❷ Turn **L** by South Pond into **The Wharf**, following bridleway beside industrial buildings and flats. Bear **R** at next waymarked junction, cross bridge and pass **cottage** on L. Keep wooden fencing on R and avoid path to L. Make for stile. Keep ahead along field boundary, keeping trees and vegetation on R. Cross 2 stiles in field corner; follow path to **R** of **polo stables**.

❸ Keep **L** and follow wooded stretch of road. Pass cottages and on reaching bend join bridle path ('Heyshott and Graffham'). Follow track as it curves to **R**.

❹ Veer **L**, just before entrance to house, and follow waymarked path as it climbs quite steeply through trees, passing between woodland and bracken. Drop down slope to waymarked path junction and turn **L** to join sandy track. Keep **L** at fork; follow track as it curves **L**, then **R**.

❺ On reaching road, turn **L** and, when it bends L by some gates, keep ahead along bridleway towards **Kennel Dairy**. Keep to **L** of outbuildings and stable blocks and walk ahead to galvanised gate. Continue on track. When it reaches field gateway, go through gate to **R** of it, following path as it runs just inside woodland.

❻ Continue along to junction, forming part of outward leg of walk, turn **R** and retrace your steps to bridge. Avoid path on L, running along to **South Pond**, and veer over to **R** to rejoin riverbank. Keep going until you reach footpath on L, leading up to ruins of St Ann's Hill. Follow path beside **Rother**, heading for kissing gate. Turn **L** and make for bridge, cross to access **Cowdray House**. After visiting house, continue along causeway path to car park.

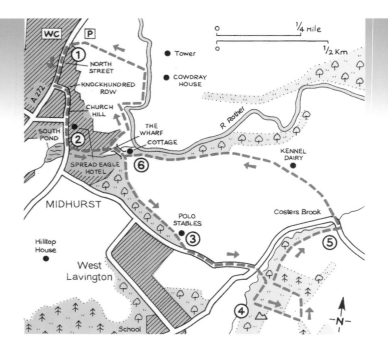

Black Down Alfred, Lord Tennyson

4½ miles (7.2km) **2hrs** **Ascent:** 315ft (95m)

Paths: Woodland paths and tracks, some minor roads

Suggested map: OS Explorer 133 Haslemere & Petersfield

Grid reference: SU 922306

Parking: Free car park off Tennyson's Lane, near Aldworth House to the southeast of Haslemere

Follow in the footsteps of the distinguished Victorian poet Alfred, Lord Tennyson on this gloriously wooded, high-level walk in the northwest corner of Sussex.

❶ Turn **L** out of car park and then **L** again to join **Sussex Border Path**. Keep **L** at junction and swing **R** at fork.

❷ Follow long distance border trail to triangular green and veer **R** here. Keep **L** at fork, still on **Sussex Border Path**, and pass over crossroads. Veer **L** just beyond it at fork and drop down to rhododendron bushes. Turn sharp **L** here and follow path through tunnel of trees.

❸ Bear **L** at drive and when, after few paces, it curves R, keep ahead through trees to join road.

❹ Turn **L** towards entrance to **Sheetland**. Avoid turning and follow lane for about 1 mile (1.6km), passing entrance to **Cotchet Farm** on L. Continue along **Fernden Lane**.

❺ Make for signposted bridleway on **L** and after few paces you reach National Trust sign ('**Black Down**'). Keep **L** here and follow sunken path as it climbs between trees, steeply in places. On higher ground, follow path as it winds pleasantly between bracken and silver birch. Walk along to seat, which takes advantage of magnificent view, partly obscured by trees. Keep seat and view on R and walk along to seat at what is known as **Temple of the Winds**.

❻ Do not retrace your steps but take path running up behind seat to junction. Don't turn **L**; instead head north on bridleway. Avoid path running off sharp R and flight of steps and veer **L** or **R** at waymarked fork. Both paths soon merge again.

❼ Continue ahead and veer **R** at next fork. Keep ahead at next junction, now following part of **Sussex Border Path** again. Veer to **R** at fork, still following long distance trail, and head for road by car park entrance.

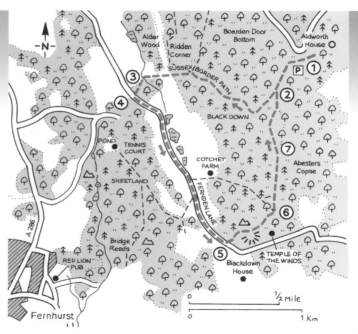

West Itchenor Harbour Sails and Trails

3½ miles (5.7km) 1hr 30min **Ascent:** Negligible

Paths: Shoreline, field tracks and paths, 1 stile
Suggested map: OS Explorer 120 Chichester, South Harting & Selsey
Grid reference: SZ 797013
Parking: Large pay-and-display car park in West Itchenor

Chichester Harbour's plentiful wildlife and colourful yachting activity form the backdrop to this waterside walk.

❶ From car park walk along to road. Bear **L**, heading towards harbour front. Pass **Ship Inn** and head to water's edge. Look for **harbour office** and **toilets** and follow footpath to **L** of **Jetty House**.

❷ Cut between hedging and fencing to reach boatyard then continue ahead on clear country path. Keep **L** at next junction; shortly path breaks cover to run hard by harbour and its expanses of mud flats. Cross **Chalkdock Marsh** and continue on waterside path.

❸ Keep going until you reach footpath sign. Turn **L**, by sturdy old oak tree, and follow path away from harbour edge, keeping to **R-H** boundary of field. Cross stile to join track on bend and continue ahead, still maintaining same direction. Pass **Itchenor Park House** on R and approach some farm outbuildings.

❹ Turn **R** by brick-and-flint farm outbuilding and follow path, soon merging with concrete track. Walk ahead to next junction and turn **L** by white gate, down to road. Bear **R** here, pass speed restriction sign and soon you reach little **Church of St Nicholas**.

❺ Follow road along to **Oldhouse Farm** then turn **L** at footpath sign to cross footbridge. Keep to **R** of several barns and follow path straight ahead across field. Pass line of trees and keep alongside ditch on **R** into next field. Path follows hedge line, making for field corner. Ahead are buildings of **Westlands Farm**.

❻ Turn sharp **L** by footpath sign and follow path across field. Skirt woodland, part of **private nature reserve**, and veer **L** at entrance to Spinney. Follow residential drive to **Harbour House**.

❼ Turn **R** just beyond it and follow path along harbour edge. Keep going along here until you reach **Itchenor Sailing Club**. Bear **L** and walk up drive to road. Opposite you should be **Ship Inn**. Turn **L** to return to car park.

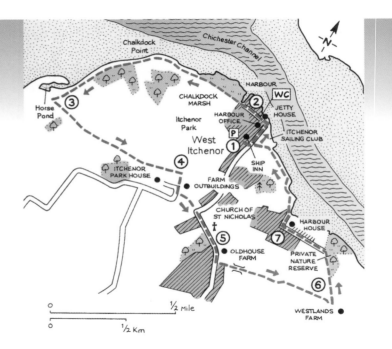

Kingley Vale Views and Yews

5 miles (8km) 2hrs **Ascent:** 440ft (134m)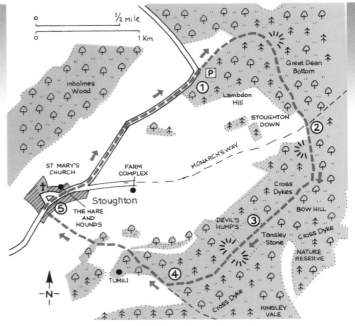

Paths: Mostly woodland paths and downland tracks

Suggested map: OS Explorer 120 Chichester, South Harting & Selsey

Grid reference: SZ 814215

Parking: Free car park at Stoughton Down

Discover a magical ancient forest teeming with wildlife high up on the South Downs.

❶ From car park make for bridleway near exit and follow it away from road, skirting dense beech woodland. There are striking views on L over pastoral, well-wooded countryside. Keep **R** at fork and follow stony path as it curves to R. Veer **R** at next waymarked fork and begin gradual ascent beneath boughs of beech trees.

❷ Eventually break cover from trees at major junction of waymarked tracks. Go straight on, looking to R for spectacular views. Continue to next bridleway sign at fork and join path running parallel to track. Cut between trees and keep going until gap on **R**. Keep to waymarked path as it runs down slope. Rejoin enclosed track, turning **L** to follow it up slope towards **Bow Hill**.

❸ On reaching **Devil's Humps**, veer off path to enjoy magnificent vistas across downland countryside.

Immediately below are trees of Kingley Vale. This was a wartime artillery range but Kingley Vale became a nature reserve in 1952 and today it is managed by English Nature. Head along footpath in westerly direction, with **nature reserve** on L. Continue between carpets of bracken and lines of beech trees.

❹ Turn **R** at next main junction and follow bridle track along field edge. On L are glimpses of Chichester Harbour, with its complex network of watery channels and sprawling mudflats. Pass several ancient burial **tumuli** then descend through area of beech woodland. Keep going until you reach road. Turn **R** and walk through pleasant village of **Stoughton**.

❺ Pass entrance to **St Mary's Church** on L, followed by **Hare and Hounds** pub. Continue through village and on R is **Monarch's Way**. Follow road out of **Stoughton**, all way to **L-H** bend where you'll see entrance to car park on Stoughton Down on **R**.

Rye Wide Skies and Lonely Seas

4½ miles (7.2km) 2hrs **Ascent:** Negligible

Paths: Level paths and good, clear tracks, no stiles

Suggested map: OS Explorer 125 Romney Marsh, Rye & Winchelsea

Grid reference: TQ 942190

Parking: Spacious free car park at Rye Harbour

Wide skies, lonely seas and lagoons form the backdrop to this remote coastal walk, which is excellent for birdwatching.

❶ Keep **Martello Tower** and entrance to holiday village on your R and enter **Rye Harbour Local Nature Reserve**. In late May and June the shingle is transformed by a colourful array of flowers. Salt marsh, vegetation along the river's edge and grazing marsh add to the variety and the old gravel pits now represent an important site for nesting terns, gulls, ducks and waders. The **Rother** can be seen on L, running parallel to path. Head for **Lime Kiln Cottage information centre** and continue on firm path, with Rother still visible on L. **Camber Sands** (popular holiday destination) nudges into view beyond river mouth.

❷ Follow path to beach, then retrace your steps to point where permissive path runs off to **L**, cutting between wildlife sanctuary areas where access is not allowed. Pass entrance to Guy Crittall hide on R. From

here enjoy superb views over **Turnery Pool**. Continue west on clear path and gradually it edges nearer shore.

❸ Ahead now is outline of old abandoned lifeboat house and, away to R in distance, unmistakable profile of **Camber Castle**. Keep going on clear path until you reach waymarked footpath on **R**, running towards line of houses on eastern edge of **Winchelsea**.

❹ Take this footpath and head inland, passing small pond on R. Glancing back, old lifeboat house can be seen. Turn **R** at next junction, pass **Watch House** and continue on track as it runs alongside several lakes. Pass to L of some dilapidated farm outbuildings and keep going along track. Lakes are still seen on L-H side, dotted with trees, and silent fishermen can often be seen along here. Begin approach to **Rye Harbour** and on L is church spire.

❺ On reaching road in centre of village, turn **L** to visit parish church before heading back along main street. Pass **Inkerman Arms** and return to car park.

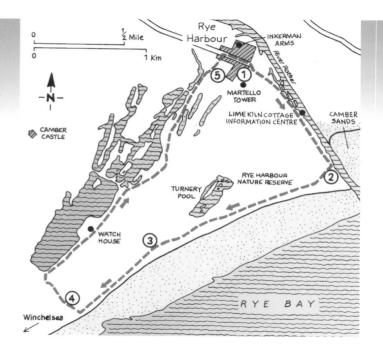

Burwash Kipling's Place

4¾ miles (7.7km) 2hrs **Ascent:** 345ft (105m)

Paths: Field and woodland paths, stretches of minor road, 16 stiles
Suggested map: OS Explorers 124 Hastings & Bexhill; 136 The Weald
Grid reference: TQ 674246 (on Explorer 124)
Parking: Free car park off A265 in Burwash village

Visit the home of Rudyard Kipling on this walk in the Dudwell Valley.

① Make for footpath behind **toilet block**, heading for stile. Follow path down slope; look for gap in trees on **R**. Cross stile at junction and continue ahead. Make for next stile and keep boundary hedge on R. Look for stile on **R** and head diagonally down field, keeping fenced spinney on R. Make for stile in field corner, follow field edge to next stile, and exit to road.

② Turn **R**; follow lane along to **Bateman's** (National Trust). Keep **L** in front of house and make for **Park Farm**. Veer **L** through gate then head up field slope, keeping trees on immediate R. Look for gate and bridleway post on **R**, passing through wood to track.

③ Bear **L**, then immediately **R**. Follow bridleway, keeping **L** at fork. Pass cottage and walk along to road. Turn **R**, eventually pass **Willingford Farm**; then climb quite steeply to small white house on R.

④ Go through kissing gate and head straight along top of field. Make for kissing gate in corner. Head diagonally **L** in next field, towards buildings of **Burnt House Farm**. Right of way leads to farm buildings and then sharply **R**, but you may find route has been diverted across paddock. Whichever, make for galvanised gate by trees and go straight ahead in next pasture, keeping wrought iron fence and farm to L.

⑤ Make for gate ahead and cross field, keeping to **L** boundary. Path cuts across next field to stile. Pass through woodland to field; head down to gap in hedge. Follow surfaced lane, which quickly becomes grassy track, passing some dilapidated farm outbuildings.

⑥ Cross stile by waymark and keep **R** here. Look for another stile shortly, turn **L** and skirt round field edge. Veer over to stile towards far end, cross footbridge; turn **L**. Follow path along to pond, pass gate and continue for few paces to track. Turn **L** and head back to **Bateman's**. Turn **R** by house. Retrace your steps back to the car park in **Burwash**.

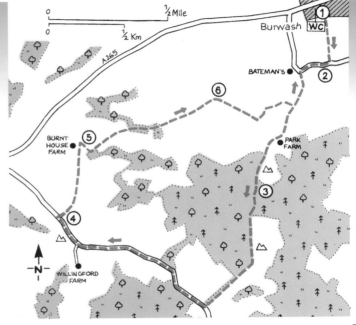

Brightling A Folly Trail

5 miles (8km) 2hrs 30min **Ascent:** 197ft (60m)

Paths: Parkland paths, woodland bridleways and lanes, 3 stiles

Suggested map: OS Explorer 124 Hastings & Bexhill

Grid reference: TQ 604209

Parking: Darwell Wood, south of Brightling, and begin at Point ④

Step into the colourful world of 'Mad Jack'
Fuller – folly-builder extraordinaire.

❶ Go through churchyard, opposite Wealden House,
to road. Turn **R**, pass **Brightling Park**; make for **L**
turning, ('Robertsbridge'). Go through kissing gate by
junction. Follow path over fields to footpath junction
and sign.

❷ Turn **R**. Follow field edge to **Tower**. Cut through
trees; descend field slope to stile and road. Bear **R**
briefly; turn **L** by barns and outbuildings. Cut between
ponds and lakes, looking for **cricket ground** by track.
The Temple can be seen on **R** at intervals. Pass
turning to farm outbuildings and continue on main
bridleway, veering **R** when it forks. Cut through area of
pheasant-rearing woodland. Make for footbridge.

❸ Turn **L** and join footpath, keeping alongside trees.
Veer away from wood when you see house on **R**. Look
for stile in boundary; make for cottage. Cross next stile
and exit to road. Turn **R** and proceed to row of

cottages. Make for parking area just beyond and look
for 2 tracks running into **Darwell Wood**.

❹ Take **L-H** bridle track, when it eventually forks,
keep **R**. Begin to swing **L** as track curves around to **R**,
still on bridleway. Keep **R** at next waymark and
continue along forest path. When it swings sharply to
R, at hairpin bend, look for bridleway sign on **L**. Follow
path through wood. On emerging, cross over pipe
linking Mountfield and Brightling gypsum mines.

❺ Follow track to **L**, then veer **R** at fork. Cross
Darwell Stream. Bear **L**, following woodland path to
road. Turn **R** to view **Darwell Reservoir** and **L** to
proceed. Follow **Kent Lane**, recross conveyor belt;
head to **Hollingrove**. On **R** is house (former chapel).

❻ Keep **L** at junction and walk along lane for short
distance, passing Glebe Cottage. Take stony track on
R and veer **L** shortly in front of part tile-hung house.
Walk to turning for **Tower**. Retrace route across fields;
follow road to **Brightling church**.

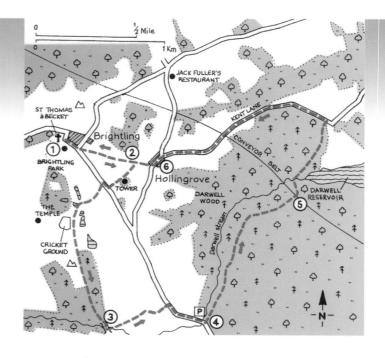

Pevensey Romans and Normans

4½ miles (7.2km) 1hr 45min **Ascent:** Negligible

Paths: Field paths, brief stretch of road and riverside, 4 stiles

Suggested map: OS Explorer 124 Hastings & Bexhill

Grid reference: TQ 645048

Parking: Pay-and-display car park by Pevensey Castle

Visit a Norman castle within a Roman fort and the eerie Pevensey Levels.

❶ On leaving car park, go straight ahead on bend, keeping Priory Court Hotel on R. **Castle** walls rise up L. Bear off to **R** just beyond hotel to follow **1066 Country Walk**.

❷ Cross **A27** and keep on trail, following sign 'Rickney'. Go through 2 gates; follow path as it bends L. Continue between fencing and hedging. Keep **Martin's Ditch** on L. Go through galvanised gate. Make for signpost and veer off diagonally **R**, leaving **1066 Country Walk** at this point.

❸ On reaching river bank footpath sign, at confluence of **Pevensey Haven** and **Chilley Stream**, continue for short distance to footbridge. Cross and aim half-**L**, making for house. Head for gap in line of bushes then go across rough, thistle-strewn ground to 2 stiles in corner by trees. Bear **R** to galvanised gate, then turn **L** and cross field, keeping house on L. On

reaching gate, turn **R** and walk along track to road.

❹ Swing **L** at lane and follow it until it curves R. Go through gate on **L**, reaching 2nd gate beyond. Follow path to gates; pass via **R-H** one. Keep ahead to gate in field corner and continue, keeping boundary on L. Make for footbridge on **L**. Cross and bear **R**. Follow edge of pasture to 2 stiles; exit to road.

❺ Keep **L** and walk along to village of **Rickney**. Avoid **1066 Country Walk** as it runs off north; cross road-bridge. Bear **L** at sign for Hankham; immediately cross bridge. Swing **L** after few paces; follow **1066 Country Walk**.

❻ Go through galvanised gate and follow path as it heads for **Pevensey Haven**. Make for another gate and continue beside or near water. On reaching gate, keep ahead and look for fingerpost, indicating path on R. Avoid path and continue ahead, still on **1066 Country Walk**. Retrace your steps to **A27**. Cross over and return to **Pevensey**.

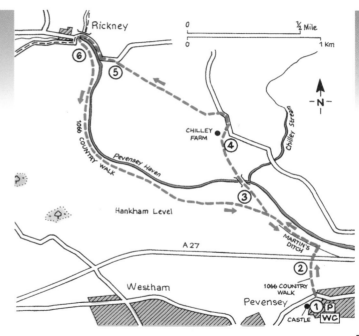

Cuckmere Haven Snake River and Seven Sisters

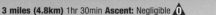

3 miles (4.8km) 1hr 30min **Ascent:** Negligible **❶**

Paths: Grassy trails and well-used paths. Mostly beside the Cuckmere or canalised branch of river

Suggested map: OS Explorer 123 South Downs Way – Newhaven to Eastbourne

Grid reference: TV 518995

Parking: Fee-paying car park at Seven Sisters Country Park

Follow a breezy trail beside the Cuckmere River as it winds in erratic fashion towards the sea.

❶ Make for gate near entrance to **Seven Sisters Country Park**. This is the focal point of the lower valley and is an amenity area of 692 acres (280ha) developed by East Sussex County Council. There are artificial lakes and park trails, and an old Sussex barn near by which has been converted to provide a visitor centre. Next follow wide, grassy path towards beach. Path gradually curves to **R**, running alongside concrete track. Cuckmere River meanders beside you, heading for open sea. Continue walking ahead between track and river and make for **South Downs Way** sign.

❷ Avoid long distance trail as it runs in from L, pass it and **Foxhole campsite** and keep ahead, through gate towards beach. Veer **L** at beach and **South Downs Way** sign. On reaching next gate, don't go

through it. Instead, keep **R** and follow beach sign. Pass couple of wartime pill boxes on L, an evocative reminder of less peaceful times, and go through gate. Join stony path and walk ahead to beach, with white wall of Seven Sisters rearing up beside you.

❸ Turn **R** and then cross shore, approaching Cuckmere Haven Emergency Point sign. Branch off to **R**, to join another track here. Follow this track for about 50yds (46m) until you come to junction and keep **L**, following Habitat Trail and Park Trail. Keep beside Cuckmere where the landscape is characterised by meandering channels and waterways, all feeding into river. Pass turning to **Foxhole campsite** and follow footpath as it veers **L**, in line with Cuckmere. Make for kissing gate and then continue on straight path alongside of river.

❹ Keep ahead to road at **Exceat Bridge** and on L is **Golden Galleon** pub. Turn **R** and follow **A259** to return to car park at **country park**.

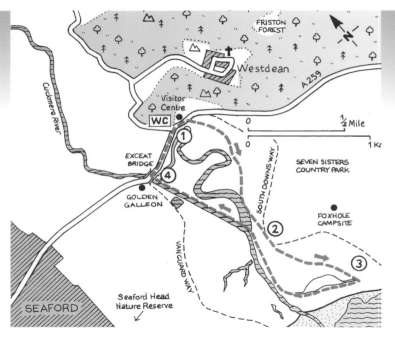

Arlington A Lakeside Trail

3 miles (4.8km) 1hr 30min **Ascent:** 82ft (25m)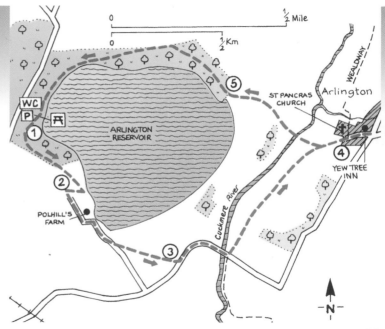
Paths: Field paths and trail, some brief road walking, 13 stiles
Suggested map: OS Explorer 123 South Down Ways – Newhaven to Eastbourne
Grid reference: TQ 528074
Parking: Arlington Reservoir

Combine a delightful walk with a little birdwatching by the Cuckmere River.

❶ From car park walk towards information boards then turn **R** to join waymarked bridleway. Cut through trees to tarmac lane; look for bridleway sign. Follow lane and soon reservoir edges into view again. On reaching gate signed ('No entry – farm access only') bear **R** and follow bridleway and footpath signs.

❷ Skirt buildings of **Polhill's Farm** and return to tarmac lane. Turn **R** and walk along to kissing gate and 'circular walk' sign. Ignore gate and keep on lane. Continue for about 100yds (91m) and then branch **L** over stile into field. Swing half-**R** and look for 2nd stile to **R** of pond. Cross 3rd stile and go across pasture to 4th stile.

❸ Turn **L** here and follow road as it bends **R**. Cross **Cuckmere River** then bear **L** to join **Wealdway**, following sign ('**Arlington**'). Walk along drive and when it curves to R, by houses, veer **L** over stile.

Arlington **church** spire can be seen now. Continue ahead, when you reach R-H fence corner, following waymark. Cross several stiles and footbridge. Keep to R of **church**, cross another stile and pass Old School on your R.

❹ Walk along lane to **Yew Tree Inn**, then retrace your steps to **church** and cross field to footbridge. Turn **R** immediately beyond it to stile in field corner. Cross pasture to obvious footbridge and continue to 2nd footbridge where there are 2 stiles. Head across field towards line of trees, following vague outline of path. **Reservoir's** embankment is clearly defined on L, as you begin gentle ascent.

❺ Cross stile by galvanised gate and go through kissing gate on immediate **R**. Follow path alongside lake and pass bird hide on L. Turn **L** further on and keep to bridleway as it reveals glimpses of lake through trees. Veer **L** at fork and follow path alongside **reservoir** and back to the start.

59

49 Firle Fine Downland Views

4¼ miles (6.8km) 2hrs **Ascent:** 476ft (145m)

Paths: Tracks, paths and roads

Suggested map: OS Explorer 123 South Down Ways – Newhaven to Eastbourne

Grid reference: TQ 468075

Parking: Free car park in Firle

Climb high above Firle Place, a Palladian mansion, and look towards distant horizons on this superb downland walk.

❶ Turn **L** out of car park, pass **Ram Inn** and follow road round to **R**, through village of **Firle**. Walk along to village stores and footpath to Charleston, once the home of Duncan Grant and Clive and Vanessa Bell, members of the Bloomsbury set. Pass turning to Firle's **Church of St Peter** and continue heading southwards, out of village.

❷ Turn **R** at junction of concrete tracks and make for road. Bear **L** then head for downland escarpment and begin long climb, which is steep in places. On reaching car park at top, swing **L** to gate and join **South Downs Way**.

❸ Head eastwards on long distance trail and, as you approach kissing gate and adjoining gate, turn sharp **L**.

❹ Follow path in northwesterly direction, down steep slopes of escarpment. On reaching wooden post, where path forks, take lower grassy path and follow it as it descends in wide sweep. Drop down to gate and walk ahead, keeping fence on **L**. Skirt around **Firle Plantation** and follow track eventually leading to junction.

❺ Bear **L** and walk along track, keeping dramatic escarpment on your **L**. As you approach village of **Firle**, track curves to **R** towards buildings of **Place Farm**. Cross over junction of concrete tracks and retrace your steps back to car park at other end of village. At the centre of the village is **Firle Place**. The house dates from the 18th century and is surrounded by glorious parkland and a backdrop of hanging woods. The estate is an example of a 'closed village' and a reminder of the autocracy of powerful landowning families. This system made it virtually impossible for outsiders to move into the village system and consequently severely regulated the development of **Firle**.

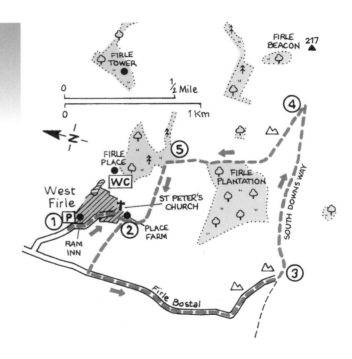

Rottingdean From the Sea to the Deans

5 miles (8km) **2hrs** **Ascent:** 305ft (92m)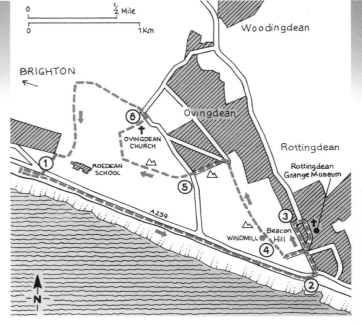

Paths: Busy village streets, downland paths and tracks, 6 stiles

Suggested map: OS Explorer 122 South Downs Way – Steyning to Newhaven

Grid reference: TQ 347032

Parking: Free car park at Roedean Bottom, at junction of A259 and B2118

Visit a picturesque village, which is famous for its artistic and literary associations.

❶ From car park cross **A259**; turn **R** towards Brighton, following paths parallel to road. Look for path on **L**; follow it down to Undercliff. Head east towards **Rottingdean**, passing café. Continue on path until reaching steps and sign ('**Rottingdean**') on **L**.

❷ Make for village; pass White Horse pub on **L**. Cross **A259** into **Rottingdean** High Street. Pass Black Horse, Nevill Road and Steyning Road; continue along street. As you approach The Green, look for The Dene on **R**.

❸ Follow road round to **R** and make for junction. Keep **R** and head back into **Rottingdean** village. Pass war memorial and village pond; look for **church** on **L**. Pass Plough Inn; walk back down to High Street. Turn **L**, then **R** into Nevill Road. Climb quite steeply; bear **R** into Sheep Walk.

❹ Keep **windmill** on **L** and follow bridleway over Downs. **Woodingdean** can be glimpsed in distance

and buildings of **Ovingdean** in foreground. Outline of **Roedean School** is visible against horizon. Continue to Longhill Road, turn **L**; proceed to junction.

❺ Cross over to stile; then head up slope to 2nd stile in R-H boundary. Bear **L** and keep going up hillside. Pass private path to **Roedean School** and continue beside wire fence to stile in field corner. Turn **R** and skirt pasture to next stile. Descend steeply towards **Ovingdean church**, cutting off field corner to reach stile. Cross into field and keep churchyard wall hard by you on **R**.

❻ Cross stile to lychgate; walk down to junction. Turn **L** then when road bends **R**, keep ahead along wide concrete track, following bridleway. Keep **L** at fork, then immediately **L** again at next fork, just beyond it. When track swings quite sharply to **L**, keep ahead along path. Pass path and stile, and car park by **A259** looms into view. When you reach road, by entrance to **Roedean School**, cross grass to car park.

Oxted North Downs Escarpment

5½ miles (8.8km) 3hrs **Ascent:** 607ft (185m) ⚠

Paths: Field edge paths, farm tracks, town roads, 12 stiles

Suggested map: OS Explorer 146 Dorking, Box Hill & Reigate

Grid reference: TQ 395529

Parking: Ellice Road car park, off Station Road East, Oxted

On the dramatic chalk downlands.

❶ Walk down Station Road East from Ellice Road car park. Turn **L** at Gresham Road then turn **R** at top into Bluehouse Lane and **L** again into Park Road. At bend, continue up signposted public footpath towards Woldingham. Cross stile beyond school playing fields, and head across field towards footbridge over **M25**.

❷ Cross **motorway**, bear **L**. Follow path to stile. Nip over and swing **L** on to **North Downs Way** National Trail. Follow waymarked trail across Chalkpit Lane and past quarry fencing, until it swings to **R** for North Downs ridge. Climb as far as waymark post beyond wicket gate and bear **L** into National Trust's Oxted Downs estate.

❸ Follow path through trees, cross stile. Turn hard **R** up rustic flight of steps. Don't miss view from seat halfway up, directly above **railway tunnel**. Swing **L** at top of steps. Follow National Trail to road at Ganger's Hill.

❹ Turn **L**, and drop back down public footpath towards **Oxted**. Join bridleway half-way down, and carry on across bridge over the **M25** on to lane past **Barrow Green Court**. Cross over **Barrow Green Road**, squeeze through wicket gate then follow footpath along edge of field past **Townland Pond** and on to Sandy Lane.

❺ Turn **R**, pass underneath **A25**. Cross Oxted High Street at **Old Bell Inn**. Follow Beadles Lane for 200yds (183m) then turn **L** into Springfield and fork off on to footpath on **R**. Drop gently down to Spring Lane, and picturesque **Oxted Mill** (privately owned).

❻ A 500yd (457m) diversion leads to **The Haycutter** pub. Cross straight over Spring Lane, zig-zag **R** and **L**, then take waymarked path through meadows to pub. Main route turns **L** past mill, and **L** again over stile at weir. Follow path through to Woodhurst Lane, and turn **L**. Fork **L** up narrow footpath at Woodhurst Park; cross **A25** into East Hill Road. At foot of the hill, turn **R** up Station Road West; then dive through station subway at top. Finally, turn **R** into Station Road East to return to start.

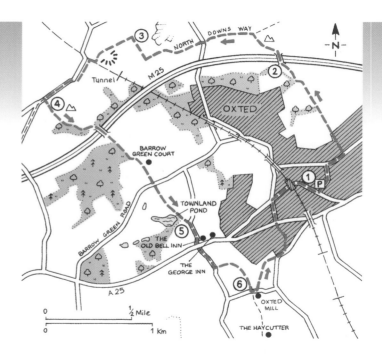

Godstone Discovering Gilbert Scott

3¾ miles (6km) 1hr 45min **Ascent:** 278ft (85m)

Paths: Footpaths and bridleways can be muddy in places, 4 stiles

Suggested map: OS Explorer 146 Dorking, Box Hill & Reigate

Grid reference: TQ 350515

Parking: Adjacent to village pond. Parking limited to 3 hours, should be plenty for this walk

On the trail of one of the leading architects of the Victorian era.

❶ Directly opposite pond in **Godstone**, take public footpath beside **White Hart** pub, signposted towards **church**. Cross Church Lane and follow path through churchyard. Keep **church** on L, and continue along winding path as it passes **Glebe Water** to yellow waymarker post at edge of open field. Turn **R** and drop down beside field to stile, then turn **L** here on to bridleway that leads under busy **A22**.

❷ Just beyond bridge, turn **R** at **Hop Garden Cottage** and follow waymarked bridleway out on to **Jackass Lane**. Turn **R** here, opposite **Little Court Farm**, now converted into private houses. At top of hill, turn **L** for 100yds (91m) to visit **St Peter's Church**. Otherwise turn **R**, and follow Tandridge Lane to public footpath just 30yds (27m) short of **Barley Mow**.

❸ Turn **R** on to waymarked **Greensand Way**, and follow broad, sandy track between open fields to

wicket gate beside **A22**. Cross main road on level, and take footpath directly opposite. Beyond small wood, 3-way wooden signpost guides you on to bridleway straight ahead. Jump tiny ford (or use footbridge) and walk up lane past **Leigh Place pond** as far as **B2236**.

❹ Leave **Greensand Way** here, and turn **R**. Follow pavement until just beyond Church Lane, then fork **L** at bus stop, up **Enterdent Road**. After 100yds (91m) turn **R** on to public footpath into woods. The waymarked path climbs, steeply in places, to stile near adventure playground on edge of **Godstone Farm**. Follow waymarked route through farm grounds, to stile just north of car park.

❺ Turn **R** on to **Tilburstow Hill** for 100yds (91m). Just beyond **Godstone Farm** delivery entrance, turn off **L** at wooden footpath signpost. Path runs briefly through farmland on edge of **Godstone** village, then leads out into **Ivy Mill Lane**. Turn **R** for short climb back to village green, then **R** again, back to car park.

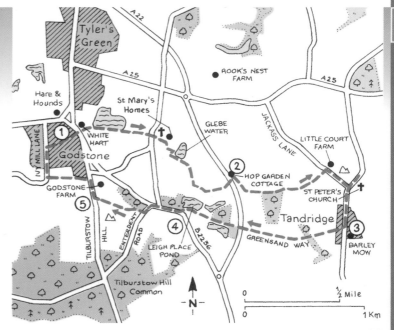

Banstead Across Chipstead Valley

3½ miles (5.7km) 2hrs **Ascent:** 295ft (90m)

Paths: Woodland and field edge paths, muddy after rain, 7 stiles

Suggested map: OS Explorer 146 Dorking, Box Hill & Reigate

Grid reference: TQ 273583

Parking: Holly Lane, Banstead

A popular woodland route.

1 Leave car park by wicket gate at top **L-H** (southeast) corner and follow waymarked gravel path. After 80yds (73m), join public footpath towards **Perrotts Farm**. Path climbs steadily through tunnel of trees along woodland edge. (Look out for old beeches on R; these may once have formed part of old boundary hedge.)

2 At 3-way wooden signpost ½ mile (800m) from car park, you have option of diversion to **Ramblers Rest**. Continue straight along permissive path, signposted towards **Fames Rough**. 200yds (183m) further on, bear **R** at another 3-way signpost, towards **Banstead Wood**. Carry on through **Fames Rough**, turn **L** on to Banstead Countryside Walk at next 3-way signpost, and follow it to waymark, 220yds (201m) further on.

3 Here Banstead Countryside Walk dives off into undergrowth on L. Keep straight ahead, nipping over fallen tree trunk few paces further on. Soon path narrows and bears to **R**, and you leave **Fames Rough** by stile at corner of open field. Follow edge of woods on your R, as far as buildings of **Perrotts Farm**.

4 Jump stile here, cross farm road, and take signposted footpath towards **Holly Lane**. Follow it along **L-H** side of field and over stile, on to gravelled farm track. Continue in same direction along edge of **Ruffett Wood**, and carry on along signposted path towards **Park Downs**. Path crosses grandly named **Chipstead Road** – little more than track – at stile, before bearing **R** and meeting **Holly Lane**.

5 Cross **Holly Lane** and nip over stile opposite, still signposted towards **Park Downs**. Follow hedgerow trees on your L until you come to stile 50yds (46m) beyond top corner of this field. Turn **L** over stile; then bear **L** along edge of **Park Downs**. Keep straight on at 4-way signpost, and follow waymarked Banstead Countryside Walk back to car park at junction of Park Road and **Holly Lane**.

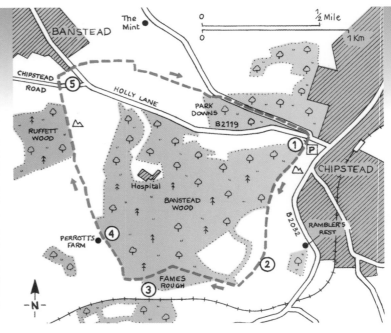

Holmwood Highwaymen and Heroes

3¼ miles (5.3km) 1hr 15min **Ascent:** 164ft (50m)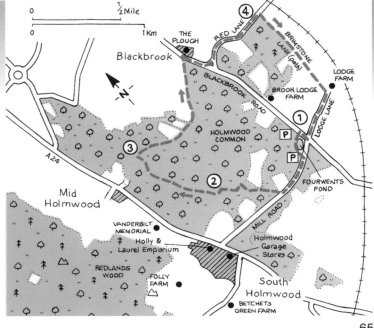

Paths: Forest and farm tracks, muddy in places, some minor roads
Suggested map: OS Explorer 146 Dorking, Box Hill & Reigate
Grid reference: TQ 183454
Parking: National Trust car park at Fourwents Pond

Once the haunt of highwaymen, American millionaire Alfred Vanderbilt also enjoyed a spot of coach driving around Holmwood.

❶ Head out of car park towards **Fourwents Pond**, and bear **R** along waterside track, keeping pond on **L**. At far corner of pond, cross small plank bridge, walk through smaller car park, and turn **R** into **Mill Road**. After 400yds (366m), turn **R** up lane ('Gable End, Applegarth and Went Cottage'). 30yds (27m) further on, fork **L** on to waymarked public footpath. Continue under set of power lines then follow blue waymarks across parting of 2 rough gravel tracks before recrossing one of them at another blue waymark. Follow path to next waymarker post and swing **L** at yellow arrow that points your way to Clematis Cottage. Turn **R** here, and join gravelled track as far as Uplands Cottage.

❷ Turn **L** for 20yds (18m), then **R** on to grassy footpath. At end of footpath turn **R**, dodge through wooden post and rail barrier; turn **L** at blue-and-yellow

waymarker post, 25yds (23m) further on. Fork **R** at next junction of paths to clearing in woods and drop down grassy slope straight ahead, now following blue waymarked route on to gravelled surface at foot of hill. After 300yds (274m), keep sharp eye out for blue-and-yellow waymarker to **L** of path, and turn **R** here, on to another gravelled path.

❸ This yellow waymarked route leads across the **Common** beside National Trust estate boundary, and brings you out opposite **Plough** pub at **Blackbrook**. Turn **R** on to **Blackbrook Road**, then **L** into **Red Lane** (signposted towards Leigh and Brockham) and follow it for about ½ mile (800m).

❹ Turn **R** into **Brimstone Lane** at public bridleway signpost. Continue through 5-bar gate and down **R-H** side of open field, leaving through 2nd gate at far end. Follow track as far as **Lodge Farm**, then turn **R** on to **Lodge Lane**, which leads back to **Fourwents Pond**. Turn **R** here, for last 100yds (91m) back to start.

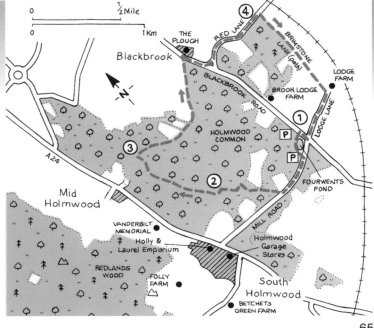

Leigh A Pastoral Scene

4 miles (6.4km) 1hr 45min **Ascent:** 73ft (22m)

Paths: Field edge and cross-field paths, 22 stiles
Suggested map: OS Explorer 146 Dorking, Box Hill & Reigate
Grid reference: TQ 223468
Parking: Lay-by between the Plough and church in Leigh

A peaceful walk through lovely scenery.

❶ With your back to **Plough**, turn **L** on to village green and take signposted footpath through churchyard and across open field to wooden footbridge. Cross brook, and waymarked stile 40yds (37m) further on; follow hedge on **R** to far corner of field. Jump stile, and turn **L** on to waymarked bridleway. After 100yds (91m), bear **R** through waymarked wicket gate towards another stile. Nip across and continue straight ahead towards far corner of field. Turn **R** over waymarked stile, and up short hill beside woods. At brow, you'll come to stile; don't jump it, but turn **R**, towards **triangulation pillar** (or trig point) across field – enjoy the views.

❷ Turn hard **L** at triangulation pillar and double back to far corner of field. You could have kept straight on beside hedge that you followed earlier, but that would have been trespassing! Cross stile in corner of field, then follow succession of waymarked stiles that lead to

Dene Farm, and then across farm drive. Bear half **R** here; cross field to plank bridge and stile. Continue through next field, and out on to **Deanoak Lane**.

❸ Turn **L**; then, just beyond double bend, turn **L** again, up lane towards **Stumblehole Farm**. Follow lane straight past **Tamworth Farm** and through small patch of woodland, then bear **L** at 3-way signpost on to concrete road. Continue past **Bury's Court School**. 55yds (50m) beyond **Keeper's Cottage**, look out for metal gate on **R**. Climb over here, and bear away beside infant **River Mole**. Follow waymarked route over wooden footbridge, and out on to **Flanchford Road**.

❹ Turn **L**, as far as **Little Flanchford Cottages**. After few paces, take footpath on **L**, and cross stile after 150yds (137m). Now bear **R** across 2 footbridges, and continue along **R-H** edge of next 3 fields. Walk diagonally to your **L** across 4th field, to small wicket gate. Turn **L** here, for last 100yds (91m) along road and back to start.

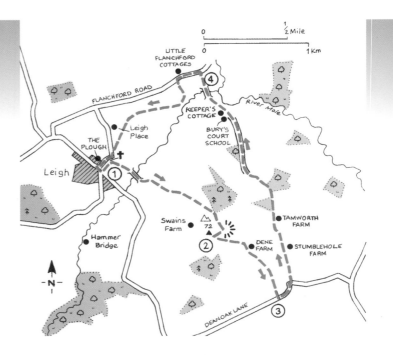

Epsom Horsing and Coursing

5 miles (8km) **2hrs** **Ascent:** 394ft (120m) ▲

Paths: Mainly broad, easy-to-follow bridleways

Suggested map: OS Explorer 146 Dorking, Box Hill & Reigate

Grid reference: TQ 223584

Parking: Car park by mini-roundabout on Tattenham Corner Rd (charges apply on race days)

A walk across Epsom Downs racecourse that everyone will enjoy.

❶ From the mini-roundabout near **Downs Lunch Box**, take signposted bridleway to Walton Road. Cross racecourse and continue along broad, waymarked lane, keeping an eye out for occasional cars. The Bridleway remains open on race days, though naturally there are some restrictions during races.

❷ At length lane swings hard **R**. Follow waymarked bridleway as it forks off down narrow path to **L**. Bear **R** at **gallops**, continuing beside rustic wooden fence before rejoining broader lane down past the **Warren** – there is a lovely view across valley from here.

❸ At bottom of hill, near ('Racehorses Only') sign, lies 6-way junction. Think of it as mini-roundabout and take 3rd exit, straight ahead. Narrow track leads through scrubby trees, but it soon leads you out between wooden posts on to broader bridleway. Turn

L and then, in a few paces, fork **L**. Keep straight on at bridleway signpost, towards **Walton on the Hill**, and follow waymarked track as it swings **R** at **Nohome Farm** and begins long climb out of valley.

❹ Bridleway ends at Cotton Mills, at junction of **Hurst Road** and **Ebbisham Lane**. Keep on down **Ebbisham Lane**, and turn **L** at bottom into Walton Street. Pass **Fox and Hounds** and **Mere Pond** then turn **L** at **The Bell** pub sign, up side of pond. After 30yds (27m), fork **R** at Withybed Corner and follow lane to **The Bell**.

❺ Keep straight on, along path signposted to Motts Hill Lane. Continue past **Coal Post** and White Cottage; then, as lane bears R, turn **L** on to bridleway. From here you simply follow waymarked route all the way back to Epsom Lane North. Journey's end is now in sight. Go across road and continue along pavement towards car park. It finishes 100yds (91m) before you reach car park, so take care.

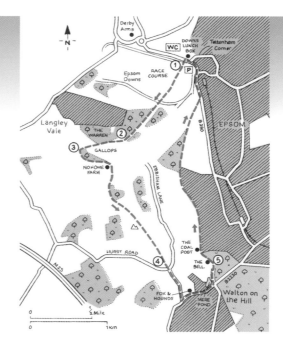

Box Hill Inventions Galore

4 miles (6.4km) 2hrs 15min **Ascent:** 803ft (245m) ⚠

Paths: Woodland tracks, with two sections on minor roads

Suggested map: OS Explorer 146 Dorking, Box Hill & Reigate

Grid reference: TQ 178513

Parking: National Trust car park, Fort Cottages, Box Hill Country Park

As well as its famous box trees, it was also the home of John Logie Baird, inventor of television.

❶ Turn **L** out of car park. **Swiss Cottage** on R (now a private house) was home to John Logie Baird during the 1920s and 30s. Cross over, and follow roadside path for ½ mile (800m). Shortly after you set out, you'll see path leading down to **viewpoint**, built in memory of Leopold Salomons of Norbury Park. The commanding views of Dorking and the Mole Valley are well worth the short diversion.

❷ Just before **Boxhills Tavern**, recross road and turn off to **L** on to signposted public bridleway. Ignore all turnings you pass, and follow signposted route as it drops down through **Juniper Bottom** to **Headley Road**.

❸ Next few hundred paces are very steep indeed. Alternatively, turn **L** on to **Headley Road**, and rejoin route by turning **L** on to **Old London Road**. This will cut out **Mickleham** village, and shorten walk by ¾ mile

(1.2km). Otherwise, cross straight over on to public footpath and steel yourself for seemingly interminable climb up long flight of rustic steps. Just beyond top of steps path bears **R** and gradient eases slightly. Soon you come to bench seat – splendid views and a good excuse for a rest. Now follow National Trust's 'long walk' waymarks as you bear **L** and drop down over footpath crossroads with **Thames Down Link**. Clamber over stile at foot of hill, and continue past church into village of **Mickleham**. Turn **L** and follow **Old London Road**. Follow pavement on **R-H** side, which at times transforms into pleasant rural path running just few paces away from road. By time you reach junction with **Zig Zag Road**, it has returned to pavement again.

❹ Cross over to junction with **Zig Zag Road**, and join signposted bridleway that climbs steadily all way back up hill to National Trust centre. Near top, you'll see old Victorian **fort** on R. Turn **R** at top of the hill for last 60yds (55m) back to car park.

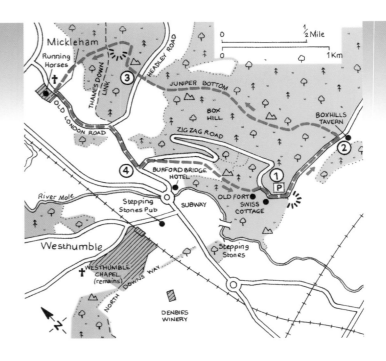

Polesden Lacey Royal Romances

4¼ miles (6.8km) 2hrs 15min **Ascent:** 607ft (185m) ⚠

Paths: Woodland and farm tracks

Suggested map: OS Explorer 146 Dorking, Box Hill & Reigate

Grid reference: TQ 141503

Parking: National Trust car park on Ranmore Common Road

A woodland walk around a country house that was once a favourite with high society.

❶ Cross road from car park, turn **L** and walk for 200yds (183m) along broad roadside verge. Turn **R** just beyond tile-hung Fox Cottages, where 2 public footpaths meet road. Take the **L-H** path through woods and, ignoring all turnings, follow it through little combe. At length it draws alongside post-and-rail fence, and veers sharp **L**. Turn **R** here, through gap in fence, and continue through woodland glade. Just beyond wooden gate, turn **L** on to signposted Yewtree Farm Walk. Continue to gravelled forest track 100yds (91m) further on, and turn **R**. Just beyond you'll come to bench seat on your **R**. There's a great view of **Polesden Lacey**, and it's a pleasant spot for a picnic.

❷ Follow gravelled track as it winds past **Yewtree Farm**; then, 150yds (137m) beyond farm, fork **L**. Follow signposted bridleway across low causeway until it climbs to meet estate road. Keep straight on, under little thatched timber footbridge. As you pass entrance to Home Farm House, look half **L** across open field. On far horizon, you'll see a long, low white building. Bear gently **R** past entrance drive to **Polesden Lacey**, and continue on to Polesden Road. Walk **R** to end of broad, grass verge on R-H side of road; then, 60yds (55m) further on, turn **R** down waymarked bridleway towards **youth hostel**.

❸ The track is relatively easy to follow now. It zigzags **R** and **L** into **Freehold Wood** and then dives under stone-arched bridge. Continue down sunken way and then bear **R** at blue waymarker post at bottom of hill and climb up gently through woods to **Tanner's Hatch**.

❹ Bear **L** at **youth hostel** and follow yellow waymarked gravel track as it climbs up gently but steadily all the way back to **Ranmore Common Road**. Turn **L** for last 200yds (183m) back to car park.

Friday Street An Ancient Landscape

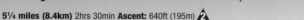

5¼ miles (8.4km) 2hrs 30min **Ascent:** 640ft (195m) ▲

Paths: Easily walked woodland tracks, but poor waymarking

Suggested map: OS Explorer 146 Dorking, Box Hill & Reigate

Grid reference: TQ 130432

Parking: Woodland parking at Starveall Corner

Through wooded sandstone heaths to the highest point in southeast England.

❶ Leave car park at gate near top **L-H** corner. After 45yds (41m), turn **L** on to woodland path and follow it to crossroads. Turn **L** and drop down to road junction. Take road towards **Abinger Common** and Wotton then, 90yds (82m) further on, turn on to narrow, unsignposted path on your **R**. Cross tarmac drive, and continue as it widens into woodland ride.

❷ Leave woods and continue briefly along **Abinger Common Road**. When you reach house called St John's, fork **R** on to bridleway and follow it through to **Friday Street**. Pass pub and **millpond**, and drop down past letter box at Pond Cottage. Follow rough track towards Wotton, bear **L** past Yew Tree Cottage, and continue until you reach gate.

❸ Turn **R** over stile, and climb sandy track into woods. Soon it levels off, bears **L** past young plantation then veers **R** at far end. Go over 2 stiles

across Sheephouse Lane, and soon you're dropping to another stile. Nip over, and follow fence across Tilling Bourne until you reach 2 steps up to stile.

❹ Cross stile, and turn **R** on to Greensand Way. It brushes road at Triple Bar Riding Centre then turns **L** on to public bridleway. Keep **R** at National Trust's Henman Base Camp, and **R** again at **Warren Farm**, where forest road ends. Here waymarked **Greensand Way** forks **R** again, along narrow woodland track. Keep ahead when you reach bench and 3-way signpost at **Whiteberry Gate**, climbing steadily at first, then more steeply, until you come to barrier and 5-way junction.

❺ Track ahead dives steeply down; turn **R**, still following waymarked **Greensand Way** as it pushes up towards **Leith Hill Tower**. Pass **tower**, taking **L-H** fork towards Starveall Corner. Follow broad track back to barrier at Leith Hill Road then swing **R** on to signposted bridleway. After 140yds (128m), turn **L** for last little stretch back to car park.

Baynards The Railway Children

4¼ miles (6.8km) 2hrs **Ascent:** 98ft (30m)

Paths: Field and forest paths, section of old railway line
Suggested map: OS Explorer 134 Crawley & Horsham
Grid reference: TQ 078349
Parking: Lay-by on Cox Green Road, Baynards, adjacent to railway bridge at start of walk

Explore the film locations of Edith Nesbit's classic children's story.

❶ From lay-by, follow Downs Link signposts down on to old railway line and head north under **Cox Green Road** bridge. Soon reach wooden gate as old line approaches **Baynards Station**. Follow **Downs Link** as it zig-zags **L** and **R**, past station buildings, and back on to old line. There is small picnic area here, information panel, and **Thurlow Arms** is on **L**. Continue for 350yds (320m), until footpath crosses line at waymarker post.

❷ Turn **R** here, nip over stile and cross open field straight ahead. Keep just to **L** of corner of woodland jutting out into field, jump waymarked stile in front, and bear gently **L** along grassy track through **Massers Wood**. Leave woods at waymarked stile, and follow field boundary on your **R**.

❸ At top corner of field, turn **R** over stile on to bridleway. Continue along surfaced lane at foot of hill, towards massive buildings of **Home Farm**. Follow lane

as it swings to **L** past farm, and continue for 80yds (73m) beyond entrance to **Brooklands Farm** on your **L**.

❹ Turn **L** here, on to gravelled track that passes back of farm and continues as grassy lane. At end of lane, carry on through 2 fields, following edge of woods on your **R** as far as buildings of **Vachery Farm**. Bear **R** here, and follow signposted bridleway until it meets farm drive at fork.

❺ Now bear **L**, signposted towards **Vachery Farm**; then, 20yds (18m) further on, fork **R** on to signposted bridleway. Bear **R** through small wood, cross wooden footbridge over **Cobbler's Brook**, and go though small gate. Now turn **R** and follow field edge as it bears around to **L** and comes to waymarked gate.

❻ Go through gate and continue straight ahead along waymarked bridleway. Follow it for 150yds (137m) then, as bridleway bears to L, dodge up to **R** and turn **L** on to **Downs Link**. Follow old railway back to **Thurlow Arms**. Retrace your steps to start.

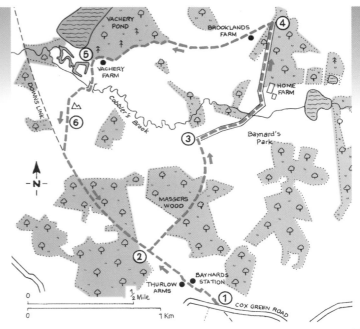

Farley Romans and Celts

5 miles (8km) 2hrs 30min **Ascent:** 574ft (175m)

Paths: Forest tracks and rutted lanes, running in water after rain

Suggested map: OS Explorer 145 Guildford & Farnham

Grid reference: TQ 051448

Parking: Forest car park (number 8) on Farley Heath

A walk through 2,000 years of history.

1 Stand in car park, facing road, and walk to entrance on R-H side. Cross road; follow signposted public bridleway across **Farley Heath**. Keep to **R** at 1st fork; continue straight across at sandy bridleway crossroads. Keep ahead at 5-way junction. Take fork to **R** few paces further on. Then, as main track swings round hard to **L**, continue ahead on waymarked woodland footpath. Path winds down to waymark post. Turn **R** here. Follow public bridleway for further 70yds (64m) to junction with **Madgehole Lane**.

2 Turn **R** and follow deeply rutted, sunken lane until it meets narrow tarmac road at tile-hung cottage.

3 Turn **L**, signposted towards Winterfold, and climb through valley past rambling, half-timbered **Madgehole Farm** to **Madgehole**. Here leave tarmac and swing hard **R**, climbing steadily past young Christmas tree plantation on **L**. Follow waymarked bridleway as it winds **R**, then **L**, through **Great Copse**

and join **Greensand Way** as it swings in from your **R**.

4 Turn **L** on to **Row Lane**. After 150yds (137m), fork **R** towards Ewhurst and Shere. Follow road over brow of hill, until you reach car park 5 on **R**. Turn **L** on to unsignposted footpath into woods; keep **R** at fork 90yds (82m) further on. Almost at once, bear **L** off main track, up narrow footpath by side of wire fence. This leads down beside garden of **Winterfold Cottage**, to another waymarker post. Fork **L**. Follow bridleway along rough cottage drive until **Row Lane**.

5 Cross over; continue on bridleway. After 200yds (183m) it bears hard **R** on to **Ride Lane**, which leads eventually to **Farley Green**. Keep **R** at junction with **Madgehole Lane**, and proceed until gradually banks roll back as you approach **Farley Green Hall Farm**.

6 Pass lovely old half-timbered farmhouse on **R**, and keep bearing **L** until you come to top of green. Bear **L** again, and follow **Farley Heath Road** for final stretch back to car park.

Pyrford A Riverside Trail

3½ miles (5.7km) 1hr 30min **Ascent:** Negligible ⓘ

Paths: Riverside tow path, some field paths and roadside

Suggested map: OS Explorer 145 Guildford & Farnham

Grid reference: TQ 039573

Parking: Unsurfaced car park at start

A charming circuit that follows the peaceful River Wey for much of the route.

❶ Walk through car park, cross bridge at traffic lights and follow roadside pavement towards **Pyrford village**. Pavement begins on **R-H** side and crosses water-meadows on several small bridges. Enjoy views of **Newark Priory** and, in wet weather, flooded fields attract swans and other waterfowl. Now pavement switches to **L-H** side, and cross **Bourne stream** bridge; then, as road swings hard R at Church Hill, keep straight on up steep woodland path to **St Nicholas Church**.

❷ Bear **R** past **church**, cross road, and take stone-flagged path through churchyard. Nip over 2 stiles at far side and follow signposted path past **Lady Place**. Bear **L** under 1st set of power lines, following field edge on R. Carry straight on past footpath turnings, **R** and **L**, as you approach 2nd set of power lines. Cross 2 stiles, and continue for 60yds (55m) to public footpath signpost directly under wires. Turn **R** and head towards corner of garden that juts out into field. Bear slightly **L** here, keeping fence on L-H side. Continue over stile at Pyrford Green House and down gravelled drive to **Warren Lane**.

❸ Zig-zag **R** and then **L** across road, then take signposted public footpath up side of open field. Carry on over small footbridge straight ahead and follow waymarked route across Pyrford Golf Course. Watch out for flying golf balls. You'll come out on to Lock Lane, just by **Pyrford Lock**. Turn **R** here and walk across bridge by **Anchor** pub.

❹ Turn **R** again, to join easy-to-follow **River Wey** tow path. Just past **Walsham Lock**, tow path zig-zags **L** and **R** across weir. Continue walking with river on your R. Cross little footbridge at **Newark Lock**. From here continue along tow path; you're now on north side of river. Beyond lock, you'll come to **Newark Lane**, take **L** turn here, and cross over **Newark Bridge** to return to car park where walk began.

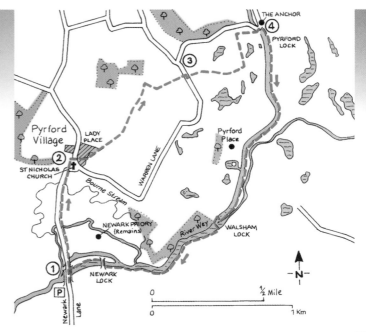

Hydon Heath National Trust's Beginnings

3¾ miles (6km) 1hr 30min **Ascent:** 344ft (105m)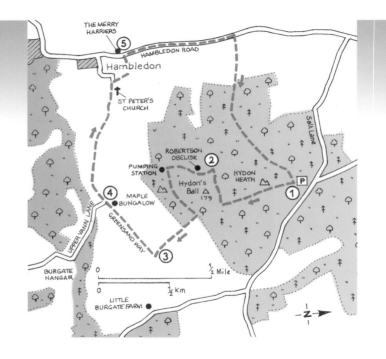

Paths: Woodland paths, farm tracks and some minor roads

Suggested map: OS Explorers 133 Haslemere & Petersfield; 145 Guildford & Farnham

Grid reference: SU 979402

Parking: National Trust car park on Salt Lane, near Hydestile

A circular walk through the varied countryside south of Godalming.

❶ Turn **L** along straight forest track just behind National Trust notice board in car park. At crest of hill, turn **R** at 8 rustic wooden posts and continue climbing for 180yds (165m) to Octavia Hill's memorial bench. Continue straight ahead, leaving bench on your L. Fork **R** between 3 large green inspection covers that give access to underground reservoirs on summit of hill, and drop down narrow path to chain link fence on edge of National Trust estate.

❷ Turn **L** here. After 60yds (55m) you'll see **Robertson obelisk** on R. The obelisk records how WA Robertson left money to the National Trust to buy this area in memory of his two brothers, who were killed in World War I. Just beyond memorial, maze of little paths will try to lead you astray. Keep as **R** as you can, and descend rutted path to forest crossroads close to small water **pumping station**. Turn **L**; then, after 200yds

(183m), fork **R** and continue to parting of ways 180m (165m) further on. Turn **R** here, and climb old sunken way as far as public bridleway marker post at top.

❸ Turn **R** here on to aptly named **Greensand Way**, and continue to **Maple Bungalow**.

❹ Pass **Maple Bungalow**, and follow **Greensand Way** through valley to **St Peter's Church, Hambledon**. 55yds (50m) beyond **church**, fork **R** at Court Farm Cottage and follow public footpath as it swings, first **R**, then **L** and drops down through sunken lane to **Hambledon Road** opposite **Merry Harriers**.

❺ Turn **R** to walk along **Hambledon Road**. Pass Feathercombe Lane and then, after 200yds (183m), turn **R** on to bridleway between open fields back towards **Hydon Heath**. Track enters woods, and you climb steeply beside deer fencing on R. Keep straight on at end of fencing and, after 100yds (91m), take middle track at 3-way junction for last 350yds (320m) to car park.

Puttenham Across the North Downs

4 miles (6.4km) 1hr 45min **Ascent:** 295ft (90m)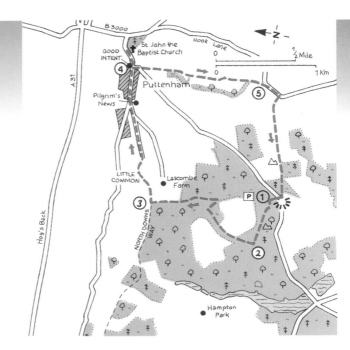

Paths: Woodland tracks and field-edge paths

Suggested map: OS Explorer 145 Guildford & Farnham

Grid reference: SU 920461

Parking: Puttenham Common top car park

A walk in the shadow of the Hog's Back.

❶ Head into view from car park, dropping down into trees with wooden handrail on R. Fork **L** through woods, and bear **R** when path forks again 100yds (91m) further on. After 150yds (137m) you'll cross another track at tiny clearing.

❷ Turn **R** here and pass green-and-mauve banded waymark post. Keep straight on until you reach 2 similar posts 300yds (274m) further on. Fork **R** here, on to narrow path that climbs gently through bracken. Continue for 25yds (23m) beyond line of electricity wires then turn **R**, on to broad sandy track. After 150yds (137m), turn sharp **L** on to similar track. Pass large white house on R, then, ignoring all turnings, follow waymarked public bridleway to junction with **North Downs Way** National Trail.

❸ Turn sharp **R** here and follow **North Downs Way** over **Little Common** and straight ahead through **Puttenham** village.

❹ Turn **R** opposite **Good Intent**, into Suffield Lane. As lane swings to R, nip over stile by public footpath signpost on **L**, and follow **L-H** edge of open field to trees on far side. Now take waymarked route over 2nd stile to **L** of the woods. 2 more stiles now lead you away from woods, keeping post and wire fence on R-H side. Cross stile beside prominent oak tree and keep straight ahead, through metal field gate. Bear **R** down short, sharp slope towards woods, and jump stile leading out on to **Hook Lane**.

❺ Turn **R**, and follow road to L-H bend. Turn **R** again, over stile by footpath sign. Cross 3 more stiles to bring you to 'right of way' waymarker. Bear **R** here, and follow fence on R. Continue to small wood, step over wooden barrier into old sunken lane, and keep straight on for 150yds (137m) to small waymark post. Turn **L** for few paces then **R** at 2nd waymark. Ascend steeply, for short way back to Suffield Lane and entrance to car park.

Chobham Common Birds and Butterflies

3 miles (4.8km) 1hr **Ascent:** 147ft (45m) ⚠

Paths: Broad bridleway tracks, can be boggy in places
Suggested map: OS Explorer 160 Windsor, Weybridge & Bracknell
Grid reference: SU 973648
Parking: Staple Hill car park, between Chobham and Longcross

An easy-to-follow circuit of Chobham's surprisingly wild and open heathland.

❶ Cross road from car park, and turn **R** on to sandy track running parallel with road on **R**.

❷ In little more than 200yds (183m) you'll rejoin road at locked barrier. Turn hard **L** here, on to waymarked horse ride that will carry you straight across middle of common. Look out for the fly agaric (*Amanita uscaria*) among the many fungi that you'll see on the common. The dome-shaped cap is the colour of tomato soup, flecked with little creamy-white scales. It is so familiar from children's books that you almost expect to see a fairy on top. There are several crossroads and turnings, but simply keep walking straight ahead until you reach **Gracious Pond Road**.

❸ Turn **L** on to road, pass thatched buildings of **Gracious Pond Farm**, and continue to sharp R-H bend. Keep straight on here, up signposted footpath. Few paces further on track bends to R; keep straight

on again, plunging into woods at wooden barrier gate and keeping **L** at fork 50yds (46m) further on.

❹ Follow path as it climbs gently through conifer plantation until, just beyond power lines, another path merges from R and you arrive at waymarker post. Follow bridleway around to **L**, cross small brook and fork **R** at next waymarker post. Now simply follow bridleway, ignoring all side turnings, until you come to waymarker post at distorted crossroads junction. Bear **R** here until, few paces beyond wooden sleeper causeway on R, you reach another waymarker post.

❺ Swing hard **L** here. Follow track as it bears around to **L** before heading straight across in an obvious line across open heath. After about 300yds (274m) take 1st waymarked footpath on **R**, and follow narrow path up through gorse and over wooden sleeper causeway. At top of the hill, you'll recognise wooden barrier just few paces from road. Cross over road, back to car park where walk began.

Witley Woodland and Follies

6 miles (9.7km) 2hrs 45min **Ascent:** 558ft (170m)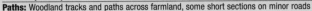

Paths: Woodland tracks and paths across farmland, some short sections on minor roads

Suggested map: OS Explorer 133 Haslemere & Petersfield

Grid reference: SU 907397

Parking: Lay-by on Dyehouse Road, 60yds (55m) west of junction with Old Portsmouth Road near Thursley

A lovely rural walk along the Greensand Way.

❶ Follow pavement towards Thursley, pass village hall. Turn **L** into The Street. When road bends **R**, turn **L** on to waymarked **Greensand Way** – signposted bridleway leads through metal gate and across field to **A3**. Cross carefully. Follow waymarked route towards Cosford Farm. As lane drops past Cosford Farm, continue along green lane to foot of hill and fork **L**. Waymarked **Greensand Way** climbs steeply through woods, crosses 2 stiles and leads to **French Lane**.

❷ Cross and continue through avenue of trees, over stile and around field edge. Half-way along side of field, dodge **L** through wicket gate. Cross drive to **Heath Hall**. Follow waymarked route to edge of **Furzefield Wood**. Turn **L** through woods, then **L** on to **Screw Corner Road**.

❸ Continue across A286. Follow **Greensand Way** until it turns off **R**, near top of hill. Keep straight on along blue waymarked bridleway to **Parsonage Farm** Cottages. Turn **L** here. Follow footpath as it zig-zags around **Parsonage Farm**. Cross farm lane. Head for stile on far side of field. Nip over and follow path through gently curving valley until 2 stiles lead past 2 white cottages. Bear **R** up cottage drive to **Roke Lane**.

❹ Turn **L**, recross A286 at **Milford Lodge**, and continue along Lea Coach Road to **Thursley Lodge**. You'll see **Witley Park** down private drive, but route lies along bridleway straight ahead. Lane drops down to junction; swing **L** past Eastlake and Lake Lodge, then bear **R** on to woodland path.

❺ Turn **L** briefly on to **French Lane**, then fork **R** on to signposted bridleway which winds through **Millhanger's** landscaped grounds and up to **A3**. Cross road. Continue on to bridleway opposite. Follow it to Old Portsmouth Road. Turn **R** then **L** into Dyehouse Road and back to lay-by at start.

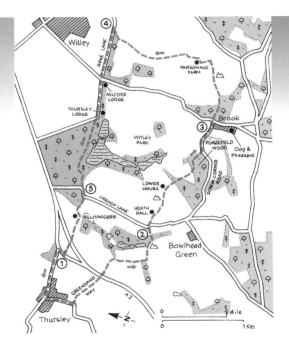

Waverley Abbey On the Pilgrim's Path

3 miles (4.8km) 1hr Ascent: 164ft (50m)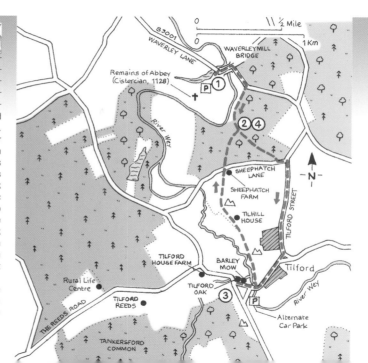

Paths: Sandy and easy to follow, two sections on minor roads

Suggested map: OS Explorer 145 Guildford & Farnham

Grid reference: SU 870455

Parking: Waverley Lane between Farnham and Elstead

By Waverley Abbey ruins in the Wey Valley.

❶ The ruins of Waverley Abbey are just at the start of the walk, a stone's throw across the fields from the car park. There was a monastic community at the abbey for over 400 years until it was suppressed by Henry VIII in 1536. Later, the buildings were quarried for stone, and many wagonloads found their way into the construction of nearby Loseley House. Turn **R** out of car park, taking care to watch out for traffic, and follow **Waverley Lane** (B3001) as it zig-zags **L** and **R** over **Waverleymill Bridge**. Continue for 200yds (183m) until road bears to L. Turn **R** here, on to public byway, and follow it through to metal gate and public byway signpost.

❷ Keep straight ahead and follow path past Friars Way Cottage until you come to **Sheephatch Lane**. Turn **L** briefly then **R** at junction with **Tilford Street** – there's no pavement for first 400yds (366m), so go carefully. Now follow road past school, over **River Wey**

bridge and on to **Tilford** village green, where you'll find **Tilford Oak** and welcome refreshment at **Barley Mow**.

❸ To continue walk, retrace your steps across river bridge. Almost at once, turn **L** at public bridleway sign just before Post Office. Path climbs gently for 500yds (457m) and brings you to tarmac lane. Turn **L**, pass **Tilhill House**, and continue up narrow sandy track straight ahead. At top of short slope, fork **R** at public bridleway waymark for 400yds (366m) climb to **Sheephatch Farm**. Cross **Sheephatch Lane**, where public byway sign points your way up gravelled track directly opposite. Track leads you through Sheephatch Copse, and soon you'll be dropping down through ancient sunken way to rejoin your outward track at metal gate and public byway signpost.

❹ Turn **L** here for easy walk back to **Waverley Lane** (B3001). Watch out for traffic as you turn **L**, then retrace your outward route over **Waverleymill Bridge** and back to car park.

Chislehurst Daylight Saving

3½ miles (5.7km) **2hrs** **Ascent: 98ft (30m)**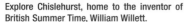

Paths: Footpaths, field edges and bridlepaths
Suggested map: OS Explorer 162 Greenwich & Gravesend
Grid reference: TQ 439708; Chislehurst rail 1 mile (1.6km)
Parking: Pay-and-display in High Street (or Queen's Head for patrons)

Explore Chislehurst, home to the inventor of British Summer Time, William Willett.

① Walk down Chislehurst High Street, past **Prick End Pond**, cross road and turn **R** into Prince Imperial Road. Follow this as it passes row of large houses and, 50yds (46m) further on, **Methodist church**. Where houses end, take bridlepath to **R**, running through trees parallel to road. Cross Wilderness Road and look L to see **memorial** to Eugene, French Prince Imperial.

② Just past golf **clubhouse** is William Willett's **Cedars** (built in 1893), identified by blue plaque. Cross road and walk up **Watts Lane** to **L** of **cricket ground**. About 150yds (137m) further on, after field, is crossroads. After few paces take narrow, tarmac path towards **St Nicholas Church**. Just before trees, turn sharp **R** and follow path to **R** of church. Exit by lychgate.

③ Walk down Hawkwood Lane to **L** of **Tiger's Head pub**. After **St Mary's Church** and **Coopers School** road bends to **L** and joins Botany Bay Lane. Continue

ahead but, when you see National Trust sign, take footpath on L into **Hawkwood Estate**, keeping to **R** of central fence. Path descends through woodland and along boardwalk that skirts edge of pond. It then climbs steadily alongside field (which may contain sheep). At top is view of **Petts Wood**.

④ At T-junction turn **L**. Follow bridlepath through wood. At **St Paul's Cray Road**, cross over; turn **L** and take path running parallel to road. After 500yds (457m) path emerges from woodland by **Graham Chiesman House**. Note village sign depicting Elizabeth I knighting Thomas Walsingham. Continue to **war memorial** by crossroads. Cross Bromley Lane.

⑤ After few paces, take footpath on **L**, just before Kemnal Road. Continue along wide track through common (you can follow pavement if this section is muddy). After you pass pond on R, cross road and follow footpath diagonally opposite through trees. Continue along Chislehurst High Street, back to start.

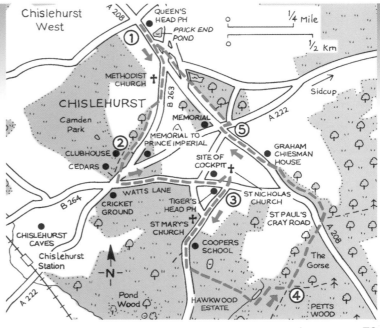

London • Southeast England

4¾ miles (7.7km) 2hrs 30min **Ascent:** Negligible **ⓘ**

Paths: Mainly lakeside tracks that can get muddy

Suggested map: OS Explorer 174 Epping Forest & Lee Valley

Grid reference: Grid reference TQ 406882; Wanstead tube

Parking: By Temple

Where Robert Dudley, Earl of Leicester, entertained Elizabeth I.

❶ Turn **L** out of **Wanstead tube** into The Green, which becomes St Mary's Avenue. At end cross road into **Overton Drive**, which runs to L of **St Mary's Church**. After Bowls and Golf Club turn **R** into The Warren Drive.

❷ At T-junction turn **L** and, almost immediately, enter **Wanstead Park** through gate opposite. Continue ahead downhill (**Florrie's Hill**) to reach ornamental water. Follow path to **L** of water and continue ahead as it runs to R of **River Roding**.

❸ After ¼ mile (400m) path swings sharply to **L** round area known as **Fortifications**, once an ammunition store and now a bird sanctuary. Soon after this path traces outline of finger-shaped section of water. To L are steep banks of **River Roding**.

❹ At meeting of paths turn **R** to continue alongside water. When path bends to **L**, you will see **Grotto** ahead.

❺ At T-junction turn **R**. At end of water turn **R** again, to cross footbridge. Take **L-H** fork towards field. At crossing of paths keep ahead until you reach **boathouse**. Turn **L** here and go out through gate.

❻ Immediately turn **R** to pick up path leading to **Heronry Pond**, which narrows and passes over mound. At crossing of paths turn **R** and keep ahead across grass. At next junction turn sharp **R**, towards trees.

❼ Path weaves around pond to reach metal gate. Go through and take **L-H** fork to join wide, grassy track lined with sweet chestnut trees. At front of **Temple** take well-defined path on **R**. Few paces further on turn **L** and continue on this path alongside **Temple**. Keep ahead, ignoring next path on R.

❽ At metal enclosure that surrounds **Grotto** turn sharp **L**, as if you going back on yourself, but, just beyond, take footpath that veers **R** and hugs water's edge before joining another, wider path. Turn next **L** up **Florrie's Hill** to retrace route back to **Wanstead tube**.

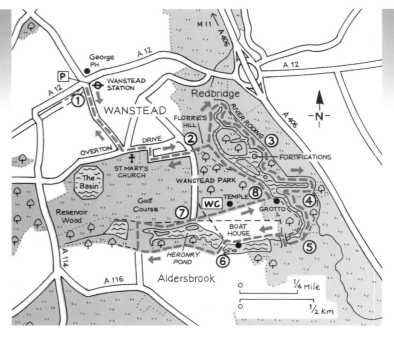

Greenwich Spending Measured Time

3½ miles (5.7km) 1hr 45min **Ascent:** 154ft (47m) ⚠️

Paths: Tarmac paths

Suggested map: OS Explorer 161 London South

Grid reference: TQ 382783 Island Gardens DLR

Discover more about the background to Greenwich Mean Time on a walk through Greenwich Park.

❶ From **Island Gardens DLR** cross over **Thames** by foot tunnel. With *Cutty Sark* on your L, cross road ahead into Greenwich Church Street. After walking another 70yds (64m) turn **L** into market. At far end turn **R** and follow King William Walk to reach **Greenwich Park**.

❷ Enter park at **St Mary's Gate** and follow wide path, known as The Avenue, as it swings to L. Continue ahead, turning **L** at toilets to reach **Royal Observatory** and superb view over London and Greenwich Royal Naval College.

❸ Retrace your steps, past **Royal Observatory's Planetarium** building and café to follow broad pathway, Blackheath Avenue. Just before **Blackheath Gate**, turn **L** through some metal gates along path that skirts edge of a large pond. (Tiny path just beyond on R leads into area for viewing deer.)

❹ Turn **R** at next fork and exit gates to enclosure. Turn **L** and take **R-H** fork. Continue along straight path beside wall.

❺ At next junction take 2nd path on your **L** and keep ahead, straight over another set of paths, to reach another junction at which **oak tree** is protected by some railings. The oak tree dates from the 12th century and is 700 years old. It is believed that Anne Boleyn danced around it with Henry VIII, and their daughter, Elizabeth, would often play in the huge hollow trunk.

❻ Turn **R**, downhill, and **R** again at next junction on path that dips and rises. Continue ahead at next set of paths and leave park at Park Row Gate. Keep ahead along Park Row, past **National Maritime Museum** and across Romney Road.

❼ At **Trafalgar Tavern** turn **L** along Thames Path to reach **Greenwich Pier**. Retrace your steps along Greenwich Foot Tunnel, built in 1902 to link Greenwich with the Isle of Dogs, to **Island Gardens DLR**.

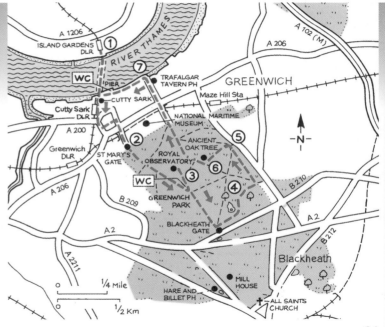

Whitechapel Guts and Garters

2¾ miles (4.4km) 1hr 30min **Ascent:** Negligible ⓪
Paths: Paved streets
Suggested map: AA Street by Street London
Grid reference: Aldgate tube

London • Southeast England

Tracing the bloody path of Jack the Ripper.

❶ With **Aldgate tube station** behind you, walk towards **St Botolph's Church** on **R**. Cross road at pedestrian lights and continue ahead, past school on corner. Turn **R** along Mitre Street. Just beyond is Mitre Square (**Catherine Eddowes, 4th victim**).

❷ Continue ahead, turning **R** into Creechurch Lane and past some posts marking boundaries of City of London. Go across 2 main roads to reach Stoney Lane. Bear **R** into Gravel Lane and, at end, past parade of shops, turn **L** along **Middlesex Street**. Take 1st **R** into Wentworth Street (Petticoat Lane).

❸ Turn **L** into Bell Lane and **R** into Brune Street. At end turn **L** and **L** again into White's Row (**Mary Jane Kelly, 5th victim**). Cross **Bell Lane** and follow Artillery Lane as it narrows to form alleyway.

❹ Turn **R** into Sandy's Row, past synagogue, then **R** and **L** to Brushfield Street. Pass **Spitalfields Market** to reach **Christ Church Spitalfields**. Cross Commercial Street at pedestrian lights. Turn **L**.

❺ As road bends turn **R** into **Hanbury Street**, find Truman's Brewery (site of **Annie Chapman, 2nd victim**). Cross Brick Lane; continue along road for another 500yds (457m), past **Brady Recreation Centre** and along alleyway.

❻ Turn **R** into main road and cross over at pedestrian lights. On **L** Durward Street (**Mary Ann Nichols, 1st victim**). Continue ahead then cross busy stream of traffic on **Whitechapel Road** into **New Road**.

❼ When you get to Fieldgate Street turn **R** towards former synagogue; then take 3rd **L** into **Settles Street**. When you reach end bear **R** and cross over at pedestrian lights, to turn **L** into **Henriques Street**. (School is site of **3rd victim, Elizabeth Stride**.)

❽ Continue ahead, following road at it swings to **R**. At end, turn **L**, then immediately **R** into Hooper Street and **R** again into **Leman Street**. Cross road into **Alie Street**. At end bear **R**, then **L** along Little Somerset Street, which comes out opposite where you began at **Aldgate tube station**.

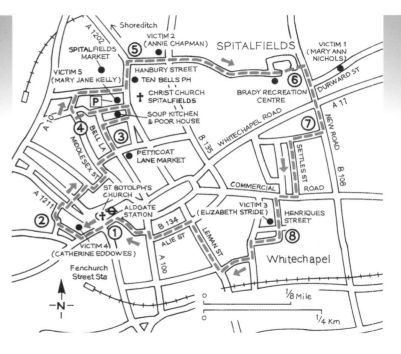

Westminster Corridors of Power

4 miles (6.4km) 2hrs 30min Ascent: Negligible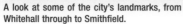

Paths: Paved streets
Suggested map: AA Street by Street London
Grid reference: Westminster tube; Farringdon tube

A look at some of the city's landmarks, from Whitehall through to Smithfield.

❶ Leave **Westminster tube** following signs to **Houses of Parliament**. Cross Abingdon Street to **Westminster Abbey** and **St Margaret's Church**. Turn back along Abingdon Street and keep ahead as road becomes Parliament Street, then **Whitehall**. Follow it past Cenotaph to **Trafalgar Square**.

❷ Turn **R** and cross Northumberland Avenue. Turn **L** into **Strand**. Turn **R** at Savoy Street, to see **Queen's Chapel of the Savoy**; otherwise proceed along **Strand**, past **Somerset House**.

❸ Turn **R** into Surrey Street, past **Roman Baths**. Turn **L** into Temple Place and **L** again on Arundel Street. After 2 churches road becomes **Fleet Street**.

❹ After Lloyds and Child & Co turn **R** into Whitefriars Street. At end turn **L** and **L** again into Dorset Rise. Take next **R** into Dorset Buildings, past **Bridewell Theatre** and along Bride Lane to **St Bride's Church**. Cross New Bridge Street.

❺ You are now in Ludgate Hill. Turn **L** into Old Bailey and continue to Central Criminal Court, **'The Old Bailey'** (on the site of the notorious former Newgate Prison). Cross Newgate Street and follow Giltspur Street to reach **St Bartholomew's Hospital**.

❻ Walk under archway to hospital, with only remaining sculpture of Henry VIII, to visit St Bartholomew-the-Less, parish church where Stuart architect Inigo Jones was baptised. As you continue past central square opposite Smithfield Market, notice marks on stone wall left by Zeppelin raid during World War I. At **St Bartholomew-the-Great** turn **L** into Hayne Street and again into Charterhouse Street.

❼ At **St John Street** turn **R** and then bear **L** into St John's Lane. Just beyond you reach St John's Gate. Keep going to reach **Grand Priory Church**, bear **L** to Jerusalem Passage, then turn **L** at end, on to Aylesbury Street. Cross Clerkenwell Street and walk along Britton Street, turning **R** into Benjamin Street to reach **Farringdon tube**.

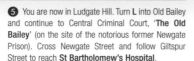

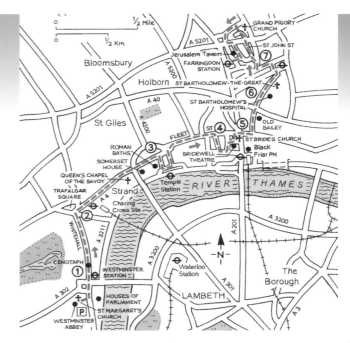

Balham On the Bright Side

3 miles (4.8km) 1hr 30min **Ascent:** 33ft (10m)
Paths: Paved streets, tarmac and gravel paths across commons
Suggested map: OS Explorer 161 London South
Grid reference: TQ 285731 Balham Station (tube and rail)

A circular route highlighting the greener spots of Balham and its most famous art deco property, Du Cane Court.

① Turn **R** at **Balham station** and then walk along Balham Station Road. Cross at lights, past **Bedford Arms pub**, into Fernlea Road. At mini-roundabout turn **R** before strip of common and pass underneath **railway** bridge. Turn **L** and then follow to wall of railway embankment, passing children's playground and playing fields on your R.

② At another bridge take **R-H** tarmac path running parallel to row of houses. As path bends to **L**, it runs alongside another **railway track** lined with trees before meeting road, Bedford Hill. Turn **R** and then cross over road to join path across **Tooting Bec Common**.

③ Turn sharp **L** and then continue along path that hugs **railway track** and passes **Tooting Bec Lido**. Pass **Lido car park** and follow path that circles it clockwise. After crossing **car park** approach road,

take **R-H** path leading on to common and, at clump of trees, turn **L** along narrow path around lake.

④ Beyond **children's playground** take next **L** to café and follow this path until you reach Hillbury Road. Turn **R** at crossroads and continue ahead into Manville Road. At next crossroads turn **L** into Ritherdon Road and continue to end.

⑤ Turn **R** at traffic lights into **Balham High Road**, passing **Du Cane Court**. This gorgeous art deco building was named after a family of Huguenots, on whose land the site was built, and designed by architect G Kay Green in the 1930s. It contains 676 flats, over 1,000 residents, and during World War II it became home to many Foreign Office staff, no doubt impressed by the short commute. If you want to see the interior of Du Cane Court you'll have to watch one of the television adaptations of Agatha Christie's Poirot, in which the lobby and flats have been featured. Then pass **St Mary's Church** before reaching **station** and start of walk.

Mayfair Laced with Luxury

2¾ miles (4.4km) 1hr 30min **Ascent:** Negligible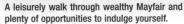

Paths: Paved streets

Suggested map: AA Street by Street London

Grid reference: Bond Street tube

A leisurely walk through wealthy Mayfair and plenty of opportunities to indulge yourself.

❶ Turn **L** outside **Bond Street tube station** and then turn sharp **L** into pedestrianised South Molton Street. At end of road turn **L** into Brook Street. Cross over road and walk along cobbled **R-H** alley, Lancashire Court, which opens out into courtyard. Just past **Hush restaurant** you'll find **Elemis Day Spa**.

❷ Turn **L** here and cross road to reach department store, **Fenwick**. Turn **R** and walk along Brook Street to reach Hanover Square. At statue of young William Pitt turn **R** into **St George Street**, walk past **St George's Church** and **L** at end on to **Conduit Street**.

❸ Take next **R** into **Savile Row**, road of fine suits. At end bear **L** and then **R** into **Sackville Street**. Turn **R** along **Piccadilly** and look out for entrance to **Albany's** courtyard.

❹ Just past auspicious-looking Burlington Arcade turn **R** into **Old Bond Street** and past several exclusive shops including those of Cartier, Mont Blanc and Tiffany. Turn **L** after Asprey & Garrard into **Grafton Street**, which takes 90-degree **L** bend, becoming Dover Street.

❺ Turn **R** along Hay Hill and then **R** again towards **Berkeley Square**, crossing 2 zebra crossings with square on your **R**, to reach Charles Street. Beyond **Chesterfield Hotel** turn **L** along Queen Street and then **R** into **Curzon Street**.

❻ Turn **R** into **South Audley Street** and its **Spy Shop**, then, at Purdey's (royal gunmakers), turn **L** into **Mount Street**. At end turn **R** along **Park Lane**, past Grosvenor House Hotel.

❼ Turn **R** into Upper Grosvenor Street, past **American Embassy** on **Grosvenor Square** and then turn **L** into **Davies Street**. Next, take 1st **R** into Brooks Mews and turn **L** along narrow Avery Row. This brings you on to Brook Street. From here, retrace your steps along South Molton Street, back to **Bond Street tube station**.

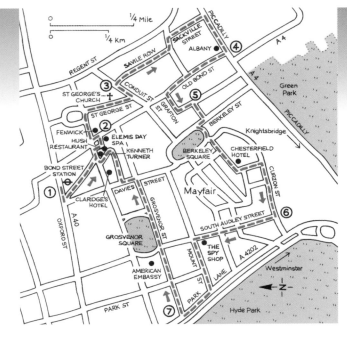

Chelsea Walking with the War Heroes

3¾ miles (6km) 2hrs **Ascent:** Negligible ⓪

Paths: Paved streets and tarmac paths
Suggested map: OS Explorer 161 London South
Grid reference: Sloane Square tube
Parking: Difficult – best to catch tube

A walk around Chelsea, home to the most famous pensioners in Britain.

❶ From **Sloane Square tube** walk ahead, crossing Lower Sloane Street. Go past Peter Jones department store and, just afterwards, on your L, **Duke of York's Headquarters**. Turn **L** into Cheltenham Terrace then bear **L** into Franklin's Row.

❷ Take 1st **R** along Royal Hospital Road. Just beyond lawns on R turn **L** into **hospital grounds** at Chelsea Gate. A few paces further on L, gravel path leads to **Great Hall, chapel and museum**. Continue to the end of road and turn **L** on to some playing fields. Now head towards **obelisk**, bear **R** and leave through gates to Chelsea Embankment.

❸ Turn **R** along Embankment and **R** into Tite Street, where Oscar Wilde once lived. At top turn **L** into Paradise Walk. Turn **R** and then sharp **L** towards Embankment and walk past **Chelsea Physic Garden**.

❹ At traffic lights cross Oakley Street and bear **R**

along narrow Cheyne Walk. Turn **R** by quirkily-named **King's Head and Eight Bells pub** into Cheyne Row. At the end turn **L** into Upper Cheyne Row. Turn **L** again into Lawrence Street – where there is a plaque to mark Chelsea Porcelain Works – then turn **R** into Justice Walk. (Don't be fooled into thinking the sign of a red-robed judge is a pub, it merely identifies where the old courthouse used to be!)

❺ Turn **L** into Old Church Street and at bottom is **Chelsea Old Church**, with statue outside of Thomas More, who worshipped here. Walk through Chelsea Embankment Gardens and cross **Albert Bridge**.

❻ At sign ('Riverside Walk'), turn **L** through gate into **Battersea Park**. Follow **Thames Path**, past **Peace Pagoda** in park, along to **Chelsea Bridge**.

❼ Turn **L** to cross bridge and continue ahead, passing **Chelsea Barracks** on R before joining Lower Sloane Street. Turn **R** to retrace your steps back to **Sloane Square tube**.

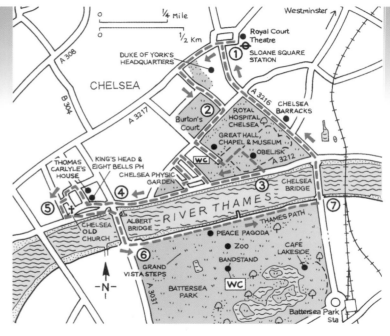

Trent Country Park A Colourful Past

3 miles (4.8km) 1hr 45min **Ascent:** 230ft (70m) ⚠

Paths: Mainly woodland tracks

Suggested map: OS Explorer 173 London North

Grid reference: TQ 283971; Cockfosters tube ¼ mile (400m)

Parking: Trent Park car park off Cockfosters Road

Take a gentle stroll around Trent Mansion, now owned by the Middlesex University.

❶ Take London Loop path to **L** of information board by café in **Trent Country Park** car park. 400yds (366m) after picnic tables, path swings to **R** and runs alongside a field. Continue for another 300yds (274m) and cross footbridge over ditch.

❷ At the end of field bear **L** beside hedgerow. To follow nature trail, enter wooden gate opposite. Otherwise, continue along path, which then dips and rejoins wider path 50yds (46m) ahead. A few paces further on, path bends to **R** above lake. Ignore next path on your **R** and continue into wood towards **Camlet Hill**.

❸ After 100yds (91m) ignore L fork and soon track widens and swings gently to **R** before passing **Hadley Road car park** (under trees).

❹ Turn **R** at junction and, a few paces further on, cross track by water tap (beware of cars heading for car park). Follow path through **Ride Wood**, as it runs parallel with bridlepath and **Hadley Road** before swinging to **R**.

❺ Go through kissing gate, cross over brook and go through another kissing gate. After walking 200yds (183m) spot house on your **L** and road, follow this for 100yds (91m).

❻ Turn **R** into **Middlesex University** car park and follow this to end. Turn **L** into box-hedged gardens (known as Wisteria Walk) and continue towards stables and clock tower on your **L**. With mansion behind you, take path to **R**, which joins wider road leading to gate. Bear **R** along this towards column in centre of mini-roundabout.

❼ Another 50yds (46m) further on, is **Pets Corner** and visitor centre with a fine selection of wooden rocking horses. Continue along this long, straight path, passing pond on L. Turn **R** along narrow path, just before stone monument, back to car park.

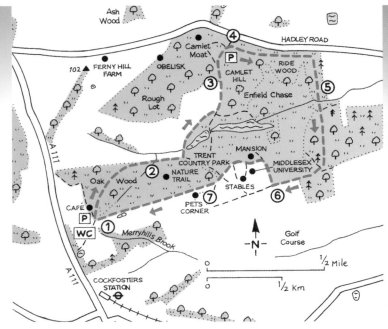

Hampstead Spring has Sprung

4¼ miles (6.8km) 2hrs **Ascent:** 344ft (105m) ▲**3**
Paths: Mainly well-trodden heathland tracks
Suggested map: OS Explorer 173 London North
Grid reference: TQ 264858 Hampstead tube
Parking: Car park off East Heath Road

Explore the heath – one of London's best-loved open spaces.

❶ Turn **L** outside **Hampstead tube** into Back Lane and into Flask Walk. Continue downhill past **Burgh House**. Follow Well Walk, passing **Wellside** on R. At East Heath Road, cross and continue on heath path.

❷ Follow tree-lined path for 200yds (183m), as far as junction and water tap. Continue for 100yds (91m); turn **L** at bench. Track narrows and zig-zags slightly before coming to gate indicating entrance to 112 acres (45ha) maintained by English Heritage.

❸ Bear **L**. Path descends gently and opens on to heathland. Follow path to **R**, on to wider track. Pass benches and proceed into woodland. If you have a dog, it should be on lead now. Pass through wooden gate along ivy-lined path, passing 2 cottages, then bear **R** towards **Kenwood House** car park. (To detour to **Spaniards Inn** take exit on to **Spaniards Road** and inn is 300yds (274m) on L.)

❹ To continue, bear **R** through car park following signs to **Kenwood House**. Turn **R**, through main gates. Take path on **R** of house, through ivy arch and on to wide terrace. Beyond **tea room** take **L** fork to pergola. Next, take path to **R**, passing metal gate.

❺ Turn **L**, downhill, passing to **L** of lake. Keep ahead through some woodland and go through another metal gate. Continue along track ahead. Take next **L** fork and head uphill. At fork take **L-H** path, which then descends. Follow tarmac path past pond.

❻ Pass 3 more **ponds**; turn sharp **R** after 3rd, along path that climbs uphill. At junction follow **R-H** path to top of **Parliament Hill**. Continue on path, through trees and between 2 **ponds**. Head uphill for 50yds (46m).

❼ Turn **L**. After 250yds (229m) bear **R** on to wider track. Follow it to East Heath Road. Cross over into Devonshire Hill; turn 1st **L** into Keats Grove to visit **Keats House**. Otherwise stay on Devonshire Hill. Turn **R** at end into Rosslyn Hill and back to start.

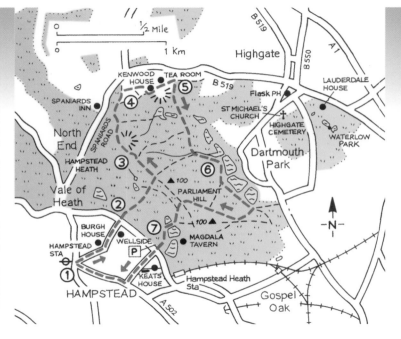

Barnes With the Wetland Birds

3¾ miles (6km) 1hr 30min **Ascent:** Negligible ⓪

Paths: Riverside tow path, muddy after rain

Suggested map: OS Explorer 161 London South

Grid reference: TQ 227767; Barnes Bridge rail ¾ mile (1.2km) or bus 283 (known as 'the Duck Bus') from Hammersmith tube

Parking: At LWC (pay if not visiting)

Explore the award-winning London Wetland Centre and join the course of the Oxford and Cambridge Boat Race.

❶ Turn **L** out of **London Wetland Centre** and follow path, initially to **L** of **Barnes Sports Centre** and then beside some sports fields. At T-junction turn **L** along well-signposted **Thames Path**, alongside river in direction of **Hammersmith Bridge**.

❷ About 100yds (91m) along path on **L** is stone post, denoting 1-mile (1.6km) marker of Oxford and Cambridge University Boat Race. Steve Fairbairn, who was born in 1862, founded Head of the River Race and this was the start of the world-famous, annual boat race that traditionally takes place in March.

❸ The landscaped area of smart flats on L is called **Waterside** and, just beyond, red-brick building bears name **Harrods Village**. Once past this, as if replicating trademark Harrods colours of green and gold, is **Hammersmith Bridge**. Continue to follow path past **St Paul's School**. On opposite side of river, Chiswick Church's green roof is visible.

❹ Turn **L** through wooden gate into **Leg of Mutton Nature Reserve**. Continue along path to R of this stretch of water, which was once a **reservoir**. When path swerves to L, leave by wooden gate to **R**. Turn **L** and then follow riverside path towards **Barnes Bridge**.

❺ Just past **Bull's Head pub** turn **L** into Barnes High Road. At next junction, by little pond, bear **L** into Church Road. Past **Sun Inn** is a row of village shops and 100yds (91m) further on, lychgate to **St Mary's Church**. At traffic lights continue ahead to return to **London Wetland Centre** (LWC). You can extend the walk by visiting the **London Wetland Centre**. There's an admission charge but once in there's lots to see and more than 2 miles (3.2km) of paths.

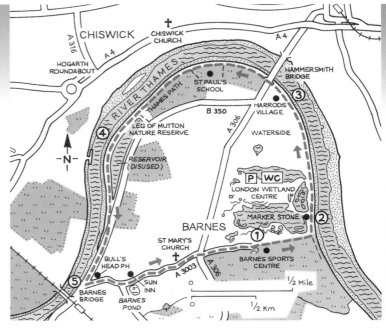

Kew Along the Thames

7½ miles (12.1km) 3hrs **Ascent:** Negligible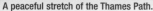
Paths: Mainly tow paths and tarmac
Suggested map: OS Explorer 161 London South
Grid reference: TQ 19276 Kew Gardens tube

London ● Southeast England

A peaceful stretch of the Thames Path.

❶ From **tube**, follow road ahead past row of shops and turn **R** along Sandycombe Road, which becomes Kew Gardens Road as it bends to L. At main road opposite **Royal Botanic Gardens**, turn **R** and continue ahead to traffic lights. Cross **Kew Green** and head towards **church** on green.

❷ Take path to **L** of **St Anne's Church** and with your back to church columns follow main path to **R**. Once across green, continue along Ferry Lane, which leads to Thames Path.

❸ Turn **L** here and follow river along path that borders Kew Gardens and offers you tempting views of the gardens from the other side of a formidable walled ditch.

❹ Just after field, cross ditch with metal gates to L, signifying boundary of **Old Deer Park**, now home of Royal Mid-Surrey Golf Course. Continue walking ahead for further mile (1.6km) on obvious track and cross **Richmond Lock** to reach other side of Thames.

❺ Follow riverside path past boatyard; follow Capital Ring path as it veers away from river, passing **Brunel University** campus. At road turn **R**. Just past **Nazareth House** convent turn **R** at mini-roundabout, ('Thames Path').

❻ Turn **L** alongside river towards **Town Wharf pub** and here, bear **L** and turn 1st **R** into Church Street. Go over bridge, past riverside London Apprentice pub. After church road swings to **L** along Park Road. Enter **Syon Park** and follow wide, tarmac road.

❼ Exit park via walled path and turn **R** at road. Cross bridge and, if this path isn't flooded, turn **R** for detour along **Grand Union Canal**. Otherwise continue along road ahead bearing **R** to go through **Watermans Park** and then rejoining Thames Path.

❽ Pass houseboats; turn **R** to cross **Kew Bridge**. Cross at pedestrian crossing; keep ahead. Turn **L** into Mortlake Road. Turn **R** into Cumberland Road and **L** at end to return along Kew Gardens Road to **Kew Gardens tube station**.

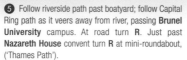

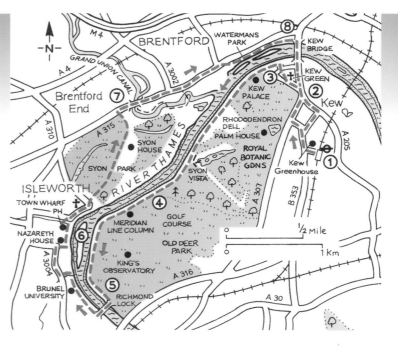

Richmond Park A Walking Safari

6¾ miles (10.9km) 2hrs 30min **Ascent:** 164ft (50m) ⚠

Paths: Mainly tarmac paths

Suggested map: OS Explorer 161 London South

Grid reference: TQ189728; Richmond Station (tube and rail) 1½ miles (2.4km)

Parking: Car park at Pembroke Lodge in Richmond Park

Enjoy a wonderful mix of panoramic views, wildlife haven and landscaped plantations, which are worthwhile seeing in all seasons.

❶ From car park at **Pembroke Lodge** turn **R** to follow **Tamsin Trail** in general direction of **Ham Gate**. Path veers to **R** and later runs close to road.

❷ At crossroads, leading to **Ham Gate**, turn **L** past **Hamcross Plantation**. At next crossroads turn **R** to visit **Isabella Plantation** (rare trees and some magnificent azaleas), otherwise continue and turn **L** at next main junction, before another plantation, and circle wood clockwise along wide track. Turn **R**, at next junction, and follow path to end of pond.

❸ Turn **R** along path between 2 **ponds** and continue ahead, ignoring paths branching off that would lead you to a car park. After this, turn **R** and follow road that swings to **L** towards **Robin Hood Gate**. Deer are often spotted here but their coats give them good camouflage, especially against the bracken.

❹ Turn **L** at **Robin Hood Gate**. Follow gravel path of **Tamsin Trail** past **Richmond Park Golf Course** and on to **Roehampton Gate**.

❺ Continue over footbridge and, after further 500yds (457m), path winds to **R** of **Adam's Pond**, which is one of the watering holes used by the deer. Follow path across upper end of park, past **Sheen Gate**, to **Richmond Gate**.

❻ Turn **L** at **Richmond Gate**. If you have time go and look for the **Henry VIII mound**, which is sited at the highest point of the park in the formal garden of Pembroke Lodge. This prehistoric burial ground is not easy to find (take higher path past cottage) but well worth the effort, for here is a view of the dome of St Paul's Cathedral 10 miles (16.1km) away. Henry VIII was said to have stood here while his second wife, Anne Boleyn, was being beheaded at the Tower of London. Retrace your steps and continue along path to reach **Pembroke Lodge** and start.

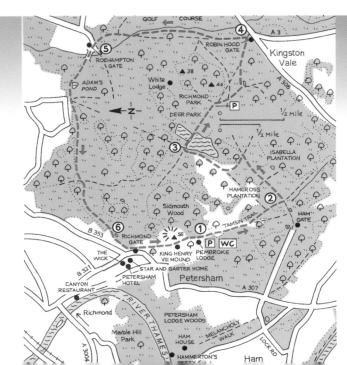

Horsenden Hill Up and Over the Hill

2¾ miles (4.4km) 1hr 30min **Ascent:** 180ft (55m)

Paths: Mainly woodland tracks

Suggested map: OS Explorer 173 London North

Grid reference: TQ 174697; add 650yds (594m) if joining the walk from Perivale tube at Point ⑤

Parking: Car park at Horsenden Hill

Some of London's best grassland and its wildlife are to be found on this walk.

① From car park walk back towards road. At metal barrier turn **R** down some steps and continue along tarmac path that runs parallel to **Horsenden Lane**. Continue in front of **Ballot Box pub** to reach tarmac path just past it.

② Turn **R** along tree-lined path; keep ahead as it passes **Ridding Wood** on L. After ¼ mile (400m) turn **R**, just before metal gate and houses, to enter **Horsenden Wood**.

③ Within few paces take **L-H** path at fork; keep ahead as it ascends then crosses tarmac path. Bear **R** at row of trees ahead that marks boundary of **golf course**. When ground levels towards top of hill, go to **viewpoint** ahead on **L**.

④ Head for **triangulation pillar** behind **viewpoint** in middle of grassy plateau. Take footpath on far **R** that leads to flight of steep, wooden steps going into thickly

wooded area. Continue down steps. At crossing of paths keep ahead, passing to **L** of oak tree, to reach road.

⑤ Turn **L** to cross footbridge over **Grand Union Canal** (Paddington Branch). Just after this, turn **L** again, down some steps, to tow path. Continue under bridge along **canal**, which later widens and passes **Perivale Wood** (and neighbouring Royal Mail depot).

⑥ Keep walking straight ahead for another ¼ mile (400m). Turn **L** after wooden footbridge to go through kissing gate. Carry on over bridge (**Horsenden Hill** is now visible again ahead) and follow winding footpath to go through another kissing gate. Turn **L** along footpath to R of some playing fields and continue ahead.

⑦ At end of fields bear **R** to go through gap in trees, then turn **L** over footbridge and keep to **R** edge of next meadow. Keep going towards another meadow and head for building beyond its L diagonal corner, **Ballot Box pub**. Cross road and turn **R** to retrace your steps along tarmac path to return to start.

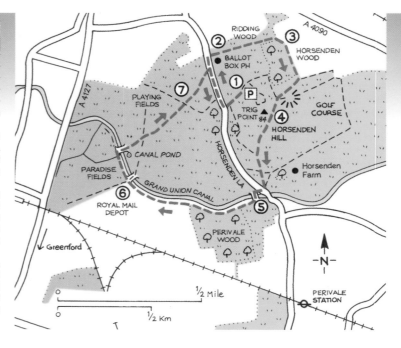

Hampton Court Anyone for Real Tennis?

4¾ miles (7.7km) 1hr 45min **Ascent:** Negligible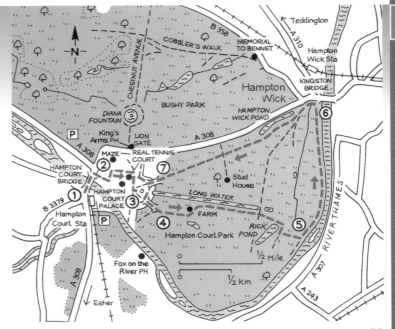

Paths: Gravel, tarmac and riverside tracks
Suggested map: OS Explorer 161 London South
Grid reference: TQ 174697 Hampton Court rail
Parking: Car park in Hampton Court Road

Discover more about the game of kings on a walk through the regal landscape of Hampton Court Park.

❶ Cross **Hampton Court Bridge**, turn **R** through main gates to **Hampton Court Palace** and walk along wide drive. Just before palace turn **L** through gatehouse and then under arch.

❷ Turn **R** just before tea room, through gateway along path through gardens. At end, on **R**, is **real tennis court** building. Pass through another gateway and turn sharp **R** to walk alongside **real tennis court** and past entrance to it. Henry VIII played real tennis here as did Charles I. Today Prince Edward and his wife Sophie are members of the 700-strong members-only club.

❸ Take central gravel path in front of palace, past fountain to railings overlooking **Long Water**, an artificial lake nearly ¾ mile (1.2km) in length. Head towards footbridge on **R** and go through wrought-iron gates.

❹ After 220yds (201m) footpath bears **L** and joins tarmac track. Follow this, turning **L** by some farm buildings, after which path runs parallel to **Long Water**. Where lake ends continue ahead at crossing of tracks and bear **R** to skirt **L** side of **Rick Pond**. Turn **L** through metal gate, along enclosed footpath and through gate to reach **River Thames**.

❺ Turn **L** along this riverside path and follow it for ¾ mile (1.2km) to **Kingston Bridge**. Here, join road leading to roundabout.

❻ At end of row of houses turn **L** through gateway. Immediately after cattle grid bear **R** along grassy path running along **L** side of boomerang-shaped **Hampton Wick Pond**. Follow straight path for about ¾ mile (1.2km) back to **Hampton Court Palace**.

❼ Bear **R** to cross footbridge and follow footpath back to real tennis court, from where you can retrace your steps to start of walk over **Hampton Court Bridge** and back into Hampton Court Road.

Harrow on the Hill Literary Highs

3½ miles (5.7km) 2hrs **Ascent:** 213ft (65m)

Paths: Footpath, fields and pavements
Suggested map: OS Explorer 173 London North
Grid reference: TQ 153880; Harrow-on-the-Hill tube
Parking: Pay-and-display in nearby streets.

Around Harrow on the Hill, where Lord Byron and Anthony Trollope went to school.

❶ Follow signs for Lowlands Road exit of **Harrow-on-the-Hill Station** and go across road at pedestrian crossing. Turn **L** and then **R**, up Lansdowne Road. At top, follow public footpath ahead ('The Hill').

❷ Before trees, turn **R** along enclosed footpath. At road turn **L**, uphill again, along tarmac path beside churchyard. (Here, you can follow crescent-shaped path to **R** and climb steep path at end, or continue ahead to reach **St Mary's Church**.)

❸ Leave by lychgate; turn **R** along Church Hill. At bottom turn sharp **L**; cross road towards school library and church. Follow road as it swings to **R** after church.

❹ Turn **R** on Football Lane and pick up footpath ('**Watford Road**'). At end of school buildings continue along path leading downhill, to reach playing fields. Look back here at Harrow School and church spires. Follow footpath sign pointing diagonally to **L** across field (not path that follows tarmac path to L) to reach stile leading to busy **Watford Road**. Cross with care.

❺ Pick up The Ducker Footpath opposite and carry on ahead as it passes close to **Northwick Park Hospital**, before veering to **R**, across grass.

❻ When you get to end of hospital buildings, turn **L** along tarmac path beside brook, with playing fields to R. At end of this long path is **Northwick Park tube**.

❼ Turn **L** just before tube station, along footpath which passes 2 chimneys. Follow this as it veers to **R** and passes between buildings of **Northwick Park Hospital** and **University of Westminster** campus. At end of footpath turn **L**. Cross at traffic lights. Turn **R** to follow dual carriageway for 100yds (91m) and go through gate along enclosed footpath running by side of **pitch-and-putt** golf course.

❽ At end of this straight, long footpath turn **R** along Peterborough Road, then **L** to reach Lowlands Road. **Harrow-on-the-Hill Station** is on your **R**.

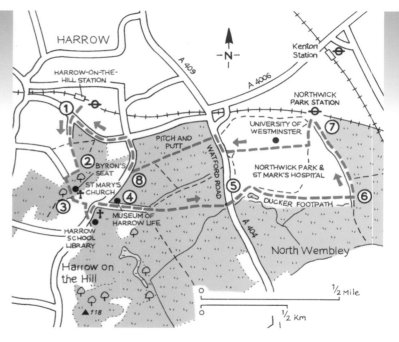

Harrow Weald No Surrender

4 miles (6.4km) 2hrs **Ascent:** 197ft (60m)

Paths: Clearly marked footpaths
Suggested map: OS Explorer 173 London North
Grid reference: TQ 158936; Stanmore tube 1½ miles (2.4km)
Parking: Car park off Warren Lane

Circling the boundaries of Bentley Priory, a key wartime defence installation.

① From car park turn **R**, along **Warren Lane**. At junction cross road and continue ahead along Priory Drive. Follow road as it bends sharply to **R**. After 50yds (43m), go through kissing gate on **L** ('Bentley Way'). Continue along track, with **Bentley Priory** to R; go through another kissing gate.

② Where another path joins at right angles, keep ahead. Fenced area on L is **deer park**. At end of fencing ignore path to L but continue ahead as track veers **L**, crosses brook, and then reaches another kissing gate before emerging on to common.

③ Continue ahead and, at crossing of paths, turn sharp **R** across common, along waymarked path. This passes through wood and then crosses footbridge, to reach row of houses. Bear **R** and follow this meandering, tree-lined track. When it joins driveway leading to farm continue towards road ahead.

④ Turn **R**. Ignore 1st footpath sign on L and take one, just beyond, along enclosed path, just before **Honeysuckle House**. Follow path. When it reaches **A409** turn **R** and take 1st **L** into Brookshill Drive.

⑤ At end of Brookshill Drive turn **R** past buildings to **Copse Farm** ('Old Redding'). Follow track then, at T-junction, turn **R**. A few paces further on, go through wooden gate on **L-H** side and continue walking ahead along footpath through wood. It swerves to **R** of gate and later runs along side of **Harrow Weald Common**.

⑥ When footpath reaches end of common turn **R** ('**Len's Avenue**'). When you get to road turn **L**. After 325yds (297m) cross over and pass through large wooden gate. Go through kissing gate and then along footpath that bisects common, with grounds to military base at **Bentley Priory** on L-H side, and Heriot's Wood down hill to R. Follow this footpath as it gently descends, before joining outward path at Point **②**. Retrace your steps to car park in **Warren Lane**.

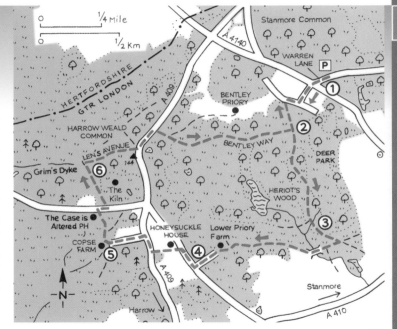

3½ miles (5.7km) 1hr 45min **Ascent:** 115ft (35m)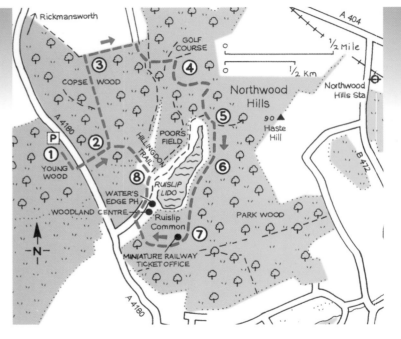
Paths: Mainly non-waymarked paths through woods
Suggested map: OS Explorer 172 Chiltern Hills East
Grid reference: TQ 080896
Parking: Young Wood car park off Ducks Hill Road

London • Southeast England

Ancient woodland, a popular lido and miniature railway.

❶ Enter **Young Wood** to R of car park. At crossing of paths turn **L** and, just before road, cross stile. Cross road with care and follow public footpath ('**Hillingdon Trail**').

❷ At wooden post turn **L** to go uphill. At T-junction turn **R** and immediately **L**, steadily downhill and over crossing of paths. Pass through barrier to wood at another T-junction.

❸ Turn **R** along straight track that borders gardens. At end, where road meets it on L, turn **R** along path that re-enters the woods. After 200yds (183m) turn **L** along path that winds through trees and ends up at kissing gate. Take path to **L** of gate, bear **L** after another gate, and cross brook to reach edge of **golf course**.

❹ Turn **R** along narrow path bordering **golf course**. Path swings to **L** and follows edge of wood. Cross footbridge over brook and bear **R** along path that skirts nature reserve.

❺ Path eventually veers **R** into **Park Wood**. Follow this uphill and keep ahead on reasonably straight path through woods. You will see track of miniature railway line to R of fence.

❻ Continue along footpath as it skirts fence, miniature railway and **lido**.

❼ Turn **R** past wooden post to **miniature railway's ticket office**. Turn **L** here, along wide path that hugs southern end of **Ruislip Lido**. Continue past children's play area and follow path round to **R**, past **Water's Edge pub** and adjacent **Woodland Centre**. From car park go through gate and pick up **Hillingdon Trail** footpath again across meadowland.

❽ At next footpath signpost turn **L** across grass and enter **Copse Wood** by wooden gate. Follow footpath as it swings round to **L** at end of some fencing. Next waymarker sign you come to is back at Point ❷. From here maintain your direction, walking ahead to retrace your footsteps back to car park.

Sandwich A Picturesque Trail

3 miles (4.8km) 1hr 30min **Ascent:** 98ft (30m) ▲

Paths: Easy town streets and field tracks, 9 stiles
Suggested map: OS Explorer 150 Canterbury & the Isle of Thanet
Grid reference: TR 351582
Parking: Behind Guildhall in Sandwich

Enjoy the quiet English charm of Sandwich on this gentle town trail.

❶ From **St Peter's Church** in town centre, walk down St Peter's Street to The Chain. Turn **R** into Galliard Street; walk to New Street. Continue to **Guildhall**. Go **L**, through car park and up to Rope Walk, where rope makers used this long, straight area to lay out their ropes.

❷ Turn **R** and, when you reach road, cross over and turn **R** down The Butts. At main road turn **L**, cross over and turn **R** up **Richborough Road**.

❸ Walk ahead, past scrapyard, and go through gate to join footpath on **R**. Follow track round, under main road and up to **railway line**. Cross stile and cross line with care, then go over 2 more stiles and on to road.

❹ Cross over, go over another stile, then walk across field to trees, heading for 3rd telegraph pole. Path now plunges into wood and up wide track. Where it splits, fork **R** and go through trees to stile.

Now follow fence line and 2 more stiles over 2 fields to join road.

❺ Cross over and walk up track ahead. **Richborough Fort** is ahead. Path runs around fort with expansive views. At bottom of track turn **R** along end of garden. Nip over stile and back over railway, leaving it by another stile. Path now leads to **R**, over neglected-looking lock and back beside river. You will eventually rejoin road, and retrace your steps to end of **Richborough Road** where you turn **L**.

❻ Go **L** through kissing gate, pass **nature reserve** and go round edge of recreation ground. Turn **R** through gate, and on to Strand Street. Turn **L**. Then **L** again in front of **Bell Hotel** and **R** past Barbican. Walk along river bank, following line of old town wall. At bend in river, turn **R** to road. Cross over, continue along footpath, pass bowling green, then turn **R** down steps into Mill Wall Place. Cross over and go back along King Street to start.

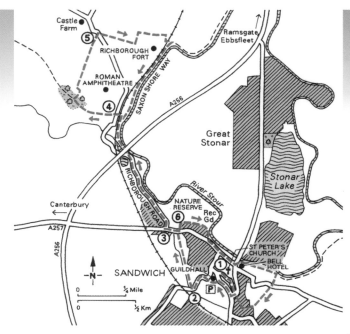

Barham An Historic Spot

4 miles (6.4km) 2hrs **Ascent:** 98ft (30m)

Paths: Village streets, tarmac tracks and field margins, 3 stiles

Suggested map: OS Explorer 138 Dover, Folkestone & Hythe

Grid reference: GR 208501

Parking: By Barham green

A walk around Barham and a pageant of history.

❶ From **Duke of Cumberland** pub by village green walk to main road, then turn **L** and walk along Valley Road – you'll get great views of 13th-century **church**, with its green-copper spire, on L-H side. Continue up Derringstone Hill, then turn **L** up Mill Lane.

❷ Take footpath on **R**, go through area of scrub, cross over road, nip over stile then go diagonally across field heading towards **R-H** edge of wood. Continue to eventually reach road.

❸ Follow road through woods. Pass 2 houses then go steeply downhill. At bottom go **L** ('Denton'). Track now opens out on **R**. Just before main road there are 2 footpaths leading off to L; take path that forks **R**.

❹ Path eventually leads into woods. Pass house, turn **L** and walk down path, with tennis courts on **R**. Turn **R** past courts and walk through grounds of 17th-century **Broome Park**, now a **hotel** and **golf club**.

Inigo Jones built the house for Sir Basil Dixwell – the man who signed the, unfulfilled, death warrant of Bonnie Prince Charlie. In the early 20th century it became the home of Lord Kitchener of Khartoum, the General who gained notoriety in World War I. He featured on the famous poster 'Your Country Needs You'. Follow path through car park then walk in front of house.

❺ Walk up track to 1st tee, cross green (look out for golf balls) and walk to marker post at trees. Turn **R** here, cross next green and go over stile into next field. Continue walking in direction of Barham church. Cross another field and come on to road, through kissing gate.

❻ Cross over to other side and walk along road almost directly ahead of you. At crossroads turn **R** and head up road, crossing stile on your **L** to follow footpath, which brings you to cemetery. Continue to road at church, turn **L**, follow road and walk back into **Barham** village centre.

Perry Wood A Crafty Walk

4 miles (6.4km) 2hrs **Ascent:** 345ft (105m) ⚠️
Paths: Woodland paths and field margins, 7 stiles
Suggested map: OS Explorer 149 Sittingbourne & Faversham
Grid reference: TQ 045556
Parking: Woodland car park in Perry Wood

A circular route through working woodland.

❶ From car park, cross road and plunge into wood, walking south along bridleway. You'll soon see evidence of recent coppicing. After few hundred paces, skirt to **L** and cross over boggy ground over boardwalk. Cross track at Keeper's Cottage gateway and bear **L** then **R**. Climb through woods, bear **L** at top and out into open heathland (it looks like woodland on OS map). Walk along ridge and climb to **observation platform** for great views.

❷ Walk past picnic area then enter orchard by stile. Continue towards bungalow at top of orchard. Skirt **L** around garden. Drop down on to tarmac lane by stile.

❸ Turn **R** to reach **Shottenden**, keep ahead at junction, pass white cottage. Continue to crossroads.

❹ Turn **L** into **Denne Manor Lane**, walk past disused oast house and continue between fields. Fork **R** under line of pylons and continue across arable fields towards telegraph pole. Maintain direction to

walk through small gate and continue past fields. Your path eventually joins rough farm track, and then bears **L** to tarmac lane at **Wytherling Court**.

❺ Turn **R** and **R** again at the next 2 T-junctions. Soon come to house and turn **L** to walk along wiggly lane. Turn **R** at main road and then join footpath on **L**.

❻ Keep ahead across open fields, aiming for lone oak tree on skyline, and walk down through 1st field, crossing barbed wire fence by broken stile. Continue over next field and sheep pasture, climbing 3 more stiles to join lane.

❼ Turn **R** on to tarmac lane, where path soon dives **L** across fields, towards Georgian house. At lane, cross then go over another field and back into wood by stile.

❽ Follow path to **L**; continue to cross lane and go through paddock. Leave this at bottom corner, then scramble through overgrown area into wood. Go through garden and on to lane. Turn **R**, return through wood. Go **L** at crossroads and back to car park.

Chilham Austen's Mr Darcy's

5 miles (8km) 2hrs 30min **Ascent:** 131ft (40m)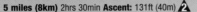

Paths: Parkland, field paths and woodland tracks, 8 stiles

Suggested map: OS Explorer 149 Sittingbourne & Faversham

Grid reference: TQ 068536

Parking: Chilham car park

A countryside ramble where Jane Austen found inspiration for 'Pride and Prejudice'.

❶ From village square, walk down School Lane and follow road past **Chilham Castle** and up to **April Cottage.** Here take footpath on the **L** – waymarker on telegraph pole.

❷ Pass between gardens, then fork **R** across field to hedge in far corner. Nip over stile and into water-meadows beside **Great Stour.** Follow hedge and continue until you reach bridge. Path bears **R** here, then takes you over narrow footbridge on to busy **A28.** Turn **L** here, walk up to **East Stour Farm,** then turn **R** and walk through farmyard, cross stile and go under **railway** bridge.

❸ Follow path ahead that bears to **L** and rises up valley. Continue ahead and follow **Stour Valley Walk** as it bears **R.**

❹ At crossing of paths, continue along **Stour Valley Walk,** go through wood, and then cross stile. Continue up field and into more woodland, where soon turn **R** to follow **Stour Valley Walk.** Descend to road crossing 2 more stiles – look back for views of **Chilham Castle.**

❺ Walk to **Woodsdale Farm** and hop over stile opposite. Walk diagonally uphill to top corner (ivy-covered trees on skyline), cross another stile and then walk short distance ahead before forking **R** along **Stour Valley Walk.** Follow this as it takes you diagonally down fields towards pair of trees in hedge. Continue in same direction and cross stile on to Eggarton Lane.

❻ Turn **R,** walk down lane, and then turn **R** again under railway and up to **A28.** Cross over and walk along lane ahead. After crossing **Great Stour,** go through gates of **College of Education** and **R** into parkland of Godmersham Park.

❼ Follow public footpath through paddocks and past house. At top corner, take footpath to **R** and walk ahead, through gate and on to road. Follow road back into **Chilham.**

Charing Pilgrims' Way

3 miles (4.8km) 1hr 30min **Ascent:** 98ft (30m) ⚠

Paths: Firm field paths and ancient trackways, 3 stiles

Suggested map: OS Explorer 137 Ashford

Grid reference: TQ 954494

Parking: Off High Street and off Station Road, Charing

A gentle circuit taking you from Charing, once a convenient stopping place for medieval pilgrims, along the ancient ridge-top track, known as Pilgrims' Way.

❶ From **church** in centre of **Charing** village, walk to High Street, cross over road and go up School Road. At roundabout turn **R** on to **A252** and then cross road to follow public footpath that leads off to **L**. Cross stile and then walk diagonally across field and through 2 metal gates. There are 2 tracks to choose from here – strike out along **L-H** track and make your way up to some trees.

❷ When you reach hedge, climb over fence, then turn **R** and walk along **Pilgrims' Way**. It's very easy going now – this route is popular with dog walkers and horse riders. Continue on track until you reach house called **Twyford**. Where track ahead forks, go to **R** and come on to **A252**. Cross over and turn **L**. Next walk about 50yds (46m) further on then turn down

Pilgrims' Way on **R-H** side. Pass tarmac track on your R and continue to reach large tree.

❸ **Pilgrims' Way** now continues ahead, eventually bringing you to **Eastwell**, the burial place of Richard Plantagenet, illegitimate son of Richard III. Unless you want to walk to **Eastwell** your route now takes you to **R**, down on to bridleway. This is an immensely atmospheric lane, with a thick canopy of trees and so old that it has sunk in the middle. Take care if it's wet, as this track is chalky and can get very slippery. At tarmac road turn **R**.

❹ Just past **Pett Farm** go over stile by green gate on **L-H** side. You will soon see **Charing church** peeping through trees. Walk towards church, crossing over another stile. At bottom of field turn **R** through gap in thick hedge that brings you out to a small hut. Walk around field, along flagstone path and past children's play area. Turn **R** up fenced path and go into churchyard and back to start.

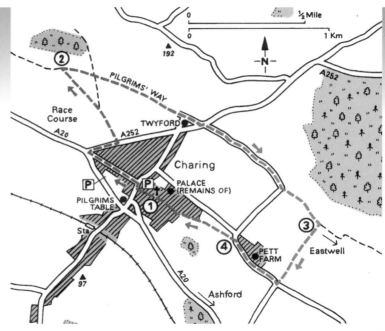

Pluckley Orchards and Perfick Villages

3 miles (4.8km) 2hrs 30min **Ascent:** 98ft (30m) ▲

Paths: Orchard tracks and footpaths, some field margins, 17 stiles

Suggested map: OS Explorer 137 Ashford

Grid reference: TQ 927454

Parking: On street in Pluckley

A ramble through countryside made famous by fictional Kentish family the Larkins, created by HE Bates.

❶ From **church**, turn **R** and head up to main road. Walk uphill, turn **R** by **Black Horse** car park sign; make for gate. Cut across playing fields and through gap in hedge into orchard. Keep ahead, keeping windbreak on R-H side, then maintain direction to cross metalled track by **Sheerland Farm**.

❷ Continue through orchards to road. Bear slightly **L**, then join footpath by brick wall. Follow this, climb stile and follow fence line on **L**, to cross 2 more stiles at bottom.

❸ Route continues ahead, through gap in wall, up to another orchard and over stile. Turn **L** now and follow track with windbreak on L. Bear **R**, go over another stile and walk towards brick wall. Turn **R** and walk through orchard to **church**. Turn **L** and go down some steps to join road opposite **Swan pub**.

❹ Turn **R**, then nip over stile on **L** and head diagonally across field – go to **L** of lone tree. Cross stile, turn **R** and walk along field edge to cross bridge and stile. Bear **L**, then **R** at end of garden to road – you'll see duck ponds on either side. Follow tarmac lane, pass house and, at waymarker, turn **L** and walk past village green of **Little Chart Forstal**.

❺ Nip over stile on **R**, then walk down **R-H** side of field, climbing 2 more stiles to reach road by **riding centre**. Turn **R**, take 1st road on **L** past farm and follow it to **Rooting Manor**.

❻ Where road bends L, cross stile by gates, turn **L** and walk along top of field. Turn **R** as you pass through windbreak and walk up track. Follow track that leads to **L** and go through orchard, eventually bearing **R** and up to **Surrenden**. Follow track on **R**, cross stile on **L** and walk up **R-H** side of field to join track. Cross stile. Continue to road and cross. Walk through orchard then over playing fields. Turn **L** and return to **church**.

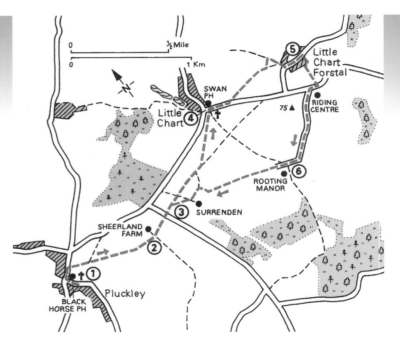

Sutton Valence Bowled Over

3½ miles (5.7km) 2hrs **Ascent:** 148ft (45m)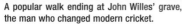

Paths: Field edges and quiet lanes, 12 stiles

Suggested map: OS Explorer 137 Ashford

Grid reference: TQ 812492

Parking: Village streets – it can get pretty crowded

A popular walk ending at John Willes' grave, the man who changed modern cricket.

❶ From **converted church** in centre of village, turn **R** down lane, then **L** at bottom to pass **ruined castle**. Continue to end of lane, and then bear **R**. Where road bears downhill, walk straight ahead along lane.

❷ Come on to surfaced area by **College Farm**. Keep walking ahead until you reach road and then turn **R**. Go downhill passing pond on R-H side. At bend, nip over stile to follow footpath on **L**.

❸ Stroll along top of field to another stile, passing pond on R-H side. Go through gap in hedge, over metal gate and on to road. Turn **L** and, after few paces, take footpath on **R**.

❹ Cross stile into field and follow fence line past tumbledown wall and up to woods ahead. Continue to some iron railings, which you follow into woods. Pass pond on your **L**, cross small bridge and continue ahead until you pop over stile into field. Bear slightly **L**,

go through gate, then head towards treeline and turn **R** to cross stile on to road.

❺ Cross road, climb another stile then continue ahead over 2 more stiles to next road. Turn **L** to follow lane uphill for 600yds (549m). Just past house turn **L** by wooden gate on to public bridleway.

❻ Your route sweeps down now, over stile and follows field edge to take you on to **Charlton Lane**. Hop over stile, cross road and walk up road ahead ('**Sutton Valence**'). Follow road past **East Sutton church** and, at another road, climb another stile into field.

❼ Take obvious path towards some trees and at waymarker go straight on along clear track. Continue to treeline in front of you, then cross stile in corner of field to join road. Walk straight on now and back to **Sutton Valence** village. To reach **St Mary's Church** walk through village, cross busy **A274** and take footpath immediately ahead. Return to village centre to finish your walk.

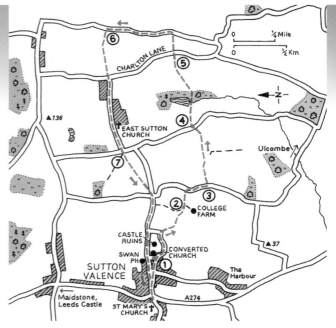

Sissinghurst Gardener's Delight

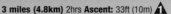

3 miles (4.8km) 2hrs **Ascent:** 33ft (10m) ▲

Paths: Well-marked field paths and woodland tracks

Suggested map: OS Explorer 137 Ashford

Grid reference: TQ 814409

Parking: On street in Frittenden

A lovely, easy walk to the famous garden created by Vita Sackville-West and Harold Nicholson.

❶ With your back to **Frittenden church** turn **R**, then **L** down pathway by hall. Cross stile and walk straight ahead over field, through gate and across another field. Go through kissing gate then straight ahead again – it's clearly marked. At gap in hedge cross little wooden bridge and head to telegraph pole. Branch **L**.

❷ Nip over stile, go across next field, over another stile and on to tarmac lane to turn **R** past **Beale Farm Oast**. At next house, turn **L** and walk up track until you pass old barn. Turn **R** just after barn, continue ahead over 2 more stiles and eventually cross footbridge to **R** of clump of trees. Walk few paces **L**, continue in same direction up edge of field then turn **L** again to cross another bridge. Scramble through some scrub and follow path ahead to another stile and on to road.

❸ Turn **R**, then **R** again at road junction. You pass **Bettenham Manor**, turn **L** up bridleway, over bridge, then pass **Sissinghurst Castle**, keeping building on L. Walk up to oast houses, then bear **L** around them, past **ticket office** and up driveway. Turn **L**, then **R** and walk by side of car parks to stile. Cross into field, then bear **R** in few paces to cross stile by some cottages.

❹ Turn **R**, walk back past cottages then bear **L** along path through trees. Continue ahead along tree-lined track. Cross stream and keep following bridleway. When you come to road, cross over and walk up **Sand Lane**.

❺ Eventually reach stile on **L-H** side, cross and then head diagonally across field to another stile in fence ahead of you. Continue diagonally, passing dip in field. Keep church spire ahead and proceed to cross another stile. Path is clear ahead, then veers to telegraph pole where you go **L**, heading for church spire. Cross bridge and walk back into village.

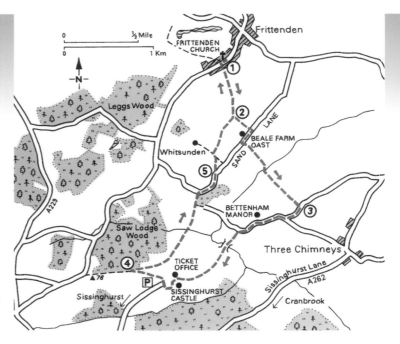

Goudhurst A Herbal High

3 miles (4.8km) 1hr 45min **Ascent:** 164ft (50m)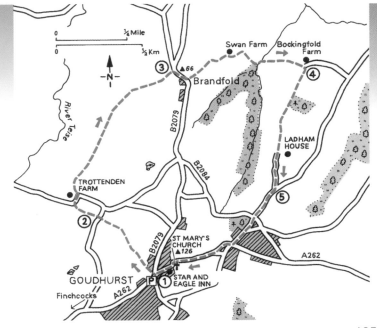

Paths: Well-marked field paths, short sections of road, 12 stiles

Suggested map: OS Explorer 136 The Weald, Royal Tunbridge Wells

Grid reference: TQ 723377

Parking: Car park in Goudhurst behind duck pond

A short but rewarding walk around one of Kent's highest villages and once the home of the Culpeper family, famous for their healing herbal remedies.

① From car park turn **L**, cross over road and walk along opposite to duck pond. Just past bus shelter turn **L** and then follow public footpath, crossing stile and walking downhill. There are outstanding views from here – the whole countryside seems to be sprinkled with oasthouses. Keep going down, past 2 large trees and walk to the bottom **R** of field where you cross over stile and on to narrow, tree-lined path. Follow this to stile. Go over little bridge and on to tarmac minor road.

② Cross over to another stile and continue ahead over pasture to tennis court. Skirt round **L** of this and, after another stile, come on to road. Turn **R**. Turn **L** through gate ('Private Road') into **Trottenden Farm**. Follow track that winds to **R**, go past pond, over stile

and walk ahead along fenced track and across pasture. Hop over stile by gate and continue ahead to another stile. At fencepost walk to **R**, round edge of meadow then cross wooden bridge, nip over another stile and into woodland. Walk uphill to another stile and continue ahead to road.

③ Turn **R** and at corner turn **L** up public bridleway. Turn **R** at cottage and come down into field. At post by hedge turn **R** and go downhill. At bottom cross some water; then veer **L**, walking uphill towards farmhouse.

④ Just before farm outbuildings turn **R** along track that runs by hedge. Eventually pass parkland of **Ladham House** on **L** then come to some concrete bollards. Continue walking to join road.

⑤ At road turn **R**, and walk up to **B2084**. Cross over and walk along road immediately ahead. At junction keep to **R** and continue to reach main road. Turn **R** here. You can now see **St Mary's Church**. Follow road and walk back into village.

Aylesford Ancient Sites

5 miles (8km) 2hrs 30min **Ascent:** 230ft (70m)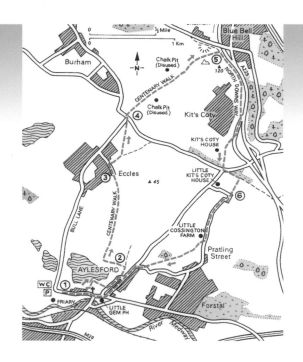

Paths: Field paths and ancient trackways, some road, 12 stiles

Suggested map: OS Explorer 148 Maidstone & the Medway Towns

Grid reference: TQ 729590

Parking: Aylesford Friary

This walk takes you to some of the most ancient sites in England.

1 From car park turn **R** towards village, cross road and join raised pathway. Ascend steps and go round by graveyard, then follow track to tarmac road. Go **L** here, then **L** again to follow **Centenary Walk**.

2 At marker post take **L-H** track and walk **L** around field until you come to scrub. Walk through this, turn **R** and walk ahead to patch of woodland. Keep this on **R** and continue ahead, ignoring any tracks on **R**. Eventually path bends **L** into **Eccles**.

3 Turn **L** along residential street then take public footpath opposite No 48. Cross stile and take **L-H** track around edge of the field. Cross 2nd stile and bear **R**, then cross 3rd stile just to **L** of electricity pylon. Keep ahead across fields, going over 5 more stiles until you reach Bull Lane.

4 Turn **R** on to Pilgrims' Way (main road) then **L** until you reach cottages. Cross over and walk up **Centenary**

Walk footpath. Follow this as it winds up to Blue Bell Hill, where there's final steep ascent. After crossing stile at top, route goes **R** along **North Downs Way**. (However, do take detour **L** to enjoy views from Blue Bell Hill.)

5 Keep following **North Downs Way** until you join road. Don't cross bridge, but continue along road. Follow sign on **R** to **Kit's Coty House** (neolithic burial chamber, which dates back 5,000 years). Walk down to busy road junction, turn **L** and join Pilgrims' Way – it's on corner, by M20 sign. (**Little Kit's Coty House**, another neolithic burial chamber is on the main road further down to the **R**.)

6 Follow lane, then take 1st track you see on **R** to reach road; follow ahead. Just past farmhouse take stile on **R** and walk diagonally across field. Cross another stile and bear **R** towards patch of woodland. Continue over another stile and find gate in bottom **R-H** corner. Go through and turn **R** along road. Turn **L** at junction, then **R** to return to start.

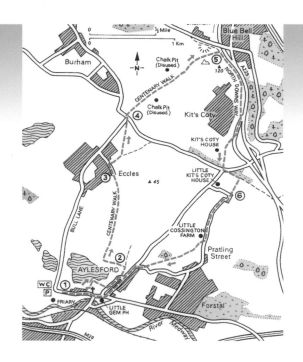

Rochester A Dickens of a Walk

6 miles (9.7km) 3hrs **Ascent:** 98ft (30m)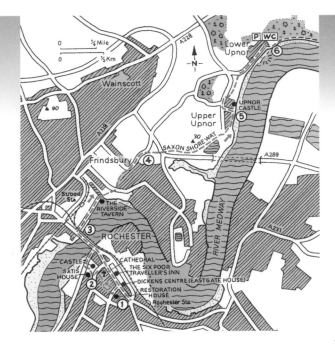
Paths: City streets and footpaths/cycleways
Suggested map: OS Explorer 163 Gravesend & Rochester
Grid reference: TQ 746682
Parking: Blue Boar car park and cathedral car park (fee)

Around Rochester's characterful streets.

❶ From Park-and-Ride point go **R** into pedestrianised part of High Street. Turn **L** up Crow Lane, then **R** by **Restoration House**, following signs ('Centenary Walk'). After crossing small park turn **R** and walk down hill to **cathedral**.

❷ Cross road and turn **L** round **castle**. Pass **Satis House**, then turn **R** and walk by **River Medway** until you reach Rochester Bridge. Cross bridge and, at traffic lights, go **R** along Canal Road, which runs under railway bridge.

❸ Walk along river, pass **Riverside Tavern** and follow footpath sign. This brings you out to new estate where you bear **R** along footpath/cycle track, which is part of **Saxon Shore Way**. Keep walking in same direction along track, which is intersected by roads at several points. At one point, pass rusting hull of a ship that could have come from the pages of a Dickens novel.

❹ At bend in road **Saxon Shore Way** bears **R**, crosses industrial land, and then finally takes you close to river bank again. At river continue walking ahead as far as entrance to **Upnor Castle**.

❺ Turn **L** along Upnor's tiny, and extremely quaint, High Street, and then go to **R**. Where road joins from **L**, keep walking ahead to join footpath that runs to **R** of main road. Follow this to **Lower Upnor**, where you turn **R** to reach quay and great views of the **Medway**. For even better views, take a short detour up the hill to your **L**. Prehistoric wild animals once roamed these slopes, as archaeological evidence shows. One of the most interesting discoveries in the area was made in 1911, when a group of Royal Engineers working near Upnor dug up the remains of a mammoth dating back to the last ice age.

❻ Retrace rotue back into **Rochester**. After crossing Rochester Bridge walk along High Street, passing sights such as **Six Poor Travellers' Inn** and **Dickens Centre**. Continue back to Park-and-Ride point.

4½ miles (7.2km) 2hrs 30min **Ascent:** 312ft (95m) ▲

Paths: Orchard tracks, field margins and footpaths, 14 stiles

Suggested map: OS Explorer 136 The Weald, Royal Tunbridge Wells

Grid reference: TQ 679418

Parking: Car park in Brenchley

This walk from Brenchley takes you back to Kent's industrial past.

❶ From car park turn **L** to war memorial. Turn **R**, then **L** at top of road and go up some steps into orchard. Walk ahead, crossing 2 stiles, then turn **L** to pass some cottages. Continue through orchard, nip over stile and on to **golf course**.

❷ Pass between greens on track, skirting corner of wood. Take track on **R**, climb stile and join road.

❸ Walk a few paces to **R** and then climb stile on **L**. Cross field and follow track to **Biggenden Farm**, where you cross stile, turn **L** and eventually reach road. Walk to **R** then take path on **L**. Cross stile and field beyond, then bear **R**. Continue towards tree line and ascend steps to **Knowle Road**.

❹ Turn **L**, then, where road bends, take path on **R**. Head across field towards hedge line, maintaining direction to cross bridge and stile. Bear **L** then **R** over another bridge and stile, to join road.

❺ Turn **R** past some hop fields, then take path on **L**. Soon turn **R** through orchard to road. Turn **L** past pond, then **R** on path at vineyard.

❻ Continue to white-timbered house, nip over stile and walk between gardens to another stile. Turn **R** to join main road, then **L** and up to parking area at **Furnace Pond**.

❼ Turn **R** at **Lake Cottage** then **R** again across bridge and walk around pond. Join path on your **R** and walk up side of orchard, to turn **R** at waymarker. Continue across lane. Turn **L** and then walk to **Hononton Farm**. Turn **R** along track, walk through orchard and then go **L** at gap in windbreak. Turn **R** at waymarker on to road.

❽ Cross over and then take track to your **L**. Follow this past house, over stile and then turn **R**. Cross over 2 more stiles and bridge. Eventually turn **R** to join road at **Halfway House pub**. Halfway up hill take track on your **R**. Cross field and return to **Brenchley**.

Tunbridge Wells Tasting the Waters

3 miles (4.8km) 1hr 30min **Ascent:** 197ft (60m) ▲

Paths: Paved streets and tarmac paths

Suggested map: OS Explorer 147 Sevenoaks & Tonbridge

Grid reference: TQ 582388

Parking: Car park behind The Pantiles

A simple trail through this elegant spa town, discovering the origins of its famous Pantiles and Royal patronage.

❶ From car park behind **The Pantiles**, turn **R** and walk up to main road. Cross over then walk up **Major York's Road**. Just after car park take footpath to **L** and walk across common, keeping ahead until you reach **Hungershall Park**. Turn **L**. Keep following road until you reach footpath that leads up to **R**.

❷ Follow path through trees, which eventually leads on to private road. Keep ahead and when you reach top take track ahead through trees. After horse barrier, bear **R**, pass churchyard, then turn **R** and walk around church and to busy main road.

❸ Turn **R** and then cross to walk to turning on **L** ('**Toad Rock**'). Path now winds uphill to rock. Now return to main road. Turn **L** and continue until you pass Fir Tree Road. On common, hidden by the trees, are Wellington Rocks.

❹ Continue along **Mount Ephraim** to cottages on R, which are built into rock. Turn **R** to walk across grass to picturesque **old house** that was once home to author William Makepeace Thackeray.

❺ Go along path that runs by **L** of house and walk along Mount Ephraim Road. This brings you out in front of pedestrianised shopping area. Turn **R** and walk down, past **museum and library** and war memorial. Turn **L** to walk up **Crescent Road** and continue until you reach **Calverley Park**, a 19th-century housing development designed by Decimus Burton. As you enter park you'll see an oak tree planted in honour of Air Chief Marshall Lord Dowding, who once lived here.

❻ Walk across Calverley Grounds to go down The Mews, then go **R** into **Grove Hill Road**. This brings you to roundabout; turn **L** and walk along **High Street**. At end go down Chapel Place, pass **Church of King Charles the Martyr**. Cross road then walk along famous **Pantiles** and back to car park.

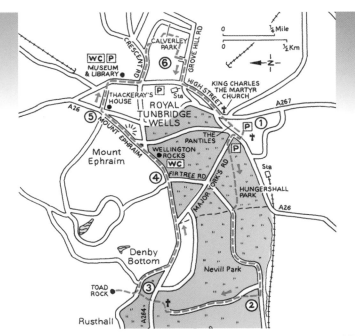

Penshurst Through Parkland

3½ miles (5.7km) 1hr 45min **Ascent:** 148ft (45m)

Paths: Broad tracks, short section on busy road, one badly signposted section by river, 2 stiles

Suggested map: OS Explorer 147 Sevenoaks & Tonbridge

Grid reference: TQ 527438

Parking: On-street parking in village, also car park for Penshurst Place

A fairly easy circular walk around the magnificent estate surrounding medieval Penshurst Place.

❶ Walk up main street of village, then turn up road opposite **Quaintways** tea room. Turn **R** at public footpath sign and cross stile. There are great views of **Penshurst Place** almost immediately. The house dates back to 1341 and the Great Hall is a fabulous example of medieval architecture. It has a timber roof, a musicians' gallery and an open hearth at its centre. There have been some notable visitors to the house over the years: Elizabeth I danced here with Robert Edward Dudley; the Black Prince ate a Christmas dinner here, and the children of Charles I came here after their father was executed. Now walk to squeeze gate, cross road, then go through another squeeze gate. Bear to **R** in direction of lake. Go through 3rd squeeze gate and, keeping lake to R, walk around it then head towards trees.

❷ Path now veers to **L** and goes uphill. Go through 2 more squeeze gates then follow signs for **Eden Valley Walk**, which leads to **R**. This is a 15-mile (24km) linear walk that traces the route of the Eden from Edenbridge to Tonbridge.

❸ Cross stile and keep walking ahead along wide, grassy track lined with trees. At end of track cut down to **R** and continue along busy road to reach sign for **Eden Valley Walk** on **R-H** side, just before bridge.

❹ Go through squeeze gate and walk through pastureland, along side of **River Medway** which is on L. Walk by river for about ¼ mile (400m), then turn **R**, away from water, and head across pasture to little bridge. Follow footpath uphill to stile that leads on to concrete track. Turn **R** and then **L** at junction.

❺ Continue walking ahead, go through gate, then down to stile. Bear **L** and walk down track. Walk under archway, then turn **R** and walk back to village.

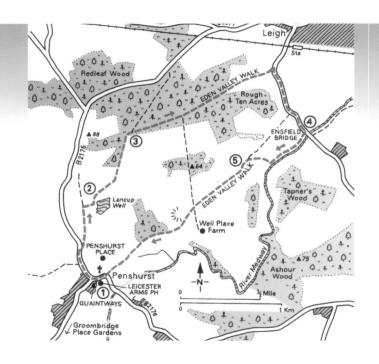

Hever Royal Passion

3½ miles (5.7km) 2hrs **Ascent:** 279ft (85m)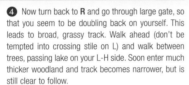

Paths: Paths, grassy tracks and field edges, some roads, 6 stiles

Suggested map: OS Explorer 147 Sevenoaks & Tonbridge

Grid reference: TQ 476448

Parking: Car park by Hever Castle

Memories of Henry VIII and Anne Boleyn on this circular walk.

① Walk under lychgate and go through churchyard following **Eden Valley Walk**. Path goes downhill, across bridge and soon becomes narrow lane parallel to road, offering occasional glimpses of lake at **Hever Castle**. The lake looks natural but was actually created by William Waldorf Astor when he bought the castle in 1903. Path now bends round, goes through woodland, across another bridge and finally opens out.

② When you come to house, climb gate following **Eden Valley Walk** (follow it all the way to Point **④**). Pass another house then take track on **R-H** side, which winds round edge of meadow to woodland. When you come to tarmac road, cross it and pop over stile.

③ Continue along enclosed track, which can get very muddy, crossing 2 more stiles and gradually heading uphill. Another stile leads you past deer fencing and through gate on to tarmac road at **Hill Hoath**.

④ Now turn back to **R** and go through large gate, so that you seem to be doubling back on yourself. This leads to broad, grassy track. Walk ahead (don't be tempted into crossing stile on L) and walk between trees, passing lake on your L-H side. Soon enter much thicker woodland and track becomes narrower, but is still clear to follow.

⑤ At branching of footpaths, bear **R**. Be warned, this can be very muddy. Continue down track, passing another 2 areas of woodland until you reach road.

⑥ Turn **R** here and walk to **Wilderness Farm**, then take road that leads to **L** opposite farm. At another road turn **R** and walk up, past road that leads to R. Continue ahead to take footpath on **R** that runs alongside **Greyhound pub**.

⑦ When you come to fork by 2 stiles turn **L**, then walk around edge of field and past pond. Continue ahead to lane, where you turn **L** then take footpath on **R**. Follow this back into **Hever**.

Walking in Safety

All these walks are suitable for any reasonably fit person, but less experienced walkers should try the easier walks first. Route finding is usually straightforward, but you will find that an Ordnance Survey map is a useful addition to the route maps and descriptions.

Risks

Although each walk has been researched with a view to minimising the risks to the walkers who follow its route, no walk in the countryside can be considered to be completely free from risk. Walking in the outdoors will always require a degree of common sense and judgement to ensure that it is as safe as possible.

- Be particularly careful on cliff paths and in upland terrain, where the consequences of a slip can be very serious.

- Remember to check tidal conditions before walking along the seashore.

- Some sections of route are by, or cross roads. Take care and remember traffic is a danger even on minor country lanes.

- Be careful around farmyard machinery and livestock, especially if you have children or a dog with you.

- Be aware of the consequences of changes of weather and check the forecast before you set off. Carry spare clothing and a torch if you are walking in the winter months. Remember that the weather can change very quickly at any time of the year, and in moorland and heathland areas, mist and fog can make route finding much harder. Don't set out in these conditions unless you are confident of your navigation skills in poor visibility. In summer remember to take account of the heat and sun; wear a hat and carry spare water.

- On walks away from centres of population you should carry a whistle and survival bag. If you do have an accident requiring the emergency services, make a note of your position as accurately as possible and dial 999.